LINEAR DESCENT

FAILURE AT FIFTY

How Alcohol And Mental Illness Nearly Destroyed Every Aspect Of My Life

First edition

This book was professionally typeset on Reedsy.
Find out more at reedsy.com

For the friends and family that have stuck with me through thick and thin, I appreciate you.

To my uncle who, when I was lost inside myself with nowhere else to go, you took me in. I'll forever hold you dear to my heart.

For those of you that can't stand me? Sorry, not sorry.

Contents

Preface

"There I was completely wasting, out of work and down."
Judas Priest (British Steel, 1980) - Breaking the Law

Disclaimer

If you can't handle fifteen minutes of a George Carlin skit without becoming offended, you should stop reading right… about… here.

Philosophy

Expect nothing and you will never be disappointed.

Apology

Due to reasons that I wasn't fully aware of until after I finished the draft of this book, I had to strip about 4 pages of a Word Document of some of the juiciest content that I was really hoping to include. Sadly, you'll have to wait for a future sequel release – which has a very indeterminate date - as it involves an agonizingly long court case process that I am growing disgusted with.

As a Child

I sit back and try to think back on my childhood, and when I do, I see more negatives than positives. Did I have a happy childhood, from other people's perspectives? I had a lot of good times. I spent most of my youth visiting with my grandparents (my biological father's parents) until we moved a little further away. I loved being with them… I was spoiled to a certain degree, and for the longest time, I felt more at home with them than I did at my home. They always gave me nice gifts for Christmas and birthdays. One year, they got me a big wheel. My grandpa also got me 2 pedal cars, which I thought were really cool. I wasn't aware of a small fact until much later which changed my perspective on what a family was for the longest time, however.

Prior to moving further away from my grandparents, I do have some vivid memories of situations at home. I remember my dad making a little snowman and us playing in the snow one winter. I remember his car collection and playing in them – pretending to be one of the Duke boys (The Dukes of Hazzard). He had a really cool green dune buggy that we'd ride around in once in a while. We had very nice neighbors that I visited frequently. They had pet raccoons, which I thought was the coolest thing, ever! One of my fondest memories of that time at home though, was running off through the woods one day to go see a sweet girl that I had a tiny crush on. It didn't end well, but I got to see her riding a horse in the field that they owned. It was a beautiful sight! Then, my dad found me, and the trip back to the house wasn't so beautiful. I can only imagine though, what was going through their minds at the time when they found out I was missing.

My grandmother on my biological father's side introduced me to coffee – Folgers Instant. I wasn't a full-blown addict at 5 years old, but I did love coffee and only got to drink it at her house. I don't think it really became a day-to-day thing until I was about 12 years old. I had found an abandoned can of Maxwell House coffee and a percolator coffee pot left behind by my stepdad's mother and decided to make a pot. I don't remember, but I think he and I both drank some that day.

I have a younger brother, who is 3 years younger than me. I only remember one time that he came with me to visit my grandparents. He wasn't impressed. He seemed to despise my grandmother for one reason or another. I couldn't figure out why and it baffled me. I couldn't imagine anyone not taking a liking to her.

I remember being afraid to go to bed. I was afraid that snakes would get into the bed and attack me or something. This foreshadows an incident later on in my life. Wait for it!

School started out great. As I said, there was a girl that I was fond of at a very early age – back when love was as innocent as it could ever be. There was another one that I remember thinking about being very beautiful, but I liked the one on the horse much more. Then, we moved away, and I wouldn't see her again until around my 5th grade year at a fair in the town where my grandma lived.

At my grandparents' house, I would get to visit relatives on that side of the family quite frequently. Every year, for a while, there would be a family reunion at one of their houses with a pasture. We'd have hayrides and fireworks and a lot of good food. Those were very good times. One year, I remember being on a hayride with one of my cousins. We had ladyfingers (tiny, but effective, red firecrackers). That was my first experience of lighting them off on my own – without supervision,

I might add. We decided to place them in cow patties. I'll leave the rest to your imagination.

One year, in summer, after school had been let out, I visited my aunt, uncle, and cousins at their home. Out of that experience, which was the first sleepover I had outside of staying with my grandparents, I remember two things. I remember playing the piano for the first time, which was prior to my experience with a recorder in school. The other memory is of my cousin and I climbing a tree in their yard. He'd commented that if he fell out of the tree, it would be my fault. I can't remember what I was doing that made him say that, but yes… he did fall out of the tree. He broke his arm and had to go to the hospital to get it placed in a cast. I felt bad, and since he said that it would be my fault if he fell, I felt as though it really was my fault. I just don't remember doing anything that would have caused him to fall in the first place. It probably ruined the rest of my stay there. I remember their road being black-topped while I was there. I don't remember much else during my stay.

His sister was beautiful. I would always anticipate their visits just to get to see her. She was a bit older, but I don't know by how much. I don't know if it would be considered strange considering her as beautiful and being a relative, but I didn't mind at the time. She recently passed away. I hadn't seen her in a very long time – since childhood, and after a while, I had grown to put that side of the family way back in the far recesses of my mind. Out of the countless relatives I would see at reunions, only a small handful of names rumble around in my head. Another strike in my history, as leaving the family in the dust was something that would become second nature to me.

I don't remember exactly when it was, but I remember only seeing my biological father in person a single time. I'd see him much later in life, but from inside a car while he and my step-dad conversed in the street - far enough away that I couldn't make out who the person was.

Grandma kept pictures of him, mostly as a child. Sometimes we'd look through her albums and when she would come across one of his photos, she'd be reminded of how much I looked like him. When I met him though, it was at a prison. I remember being in a rather small gray brick room with a door that had a narrow window where I could see his face. I don't remember speaking a word to him. It was eerie and cold. I don't even remember if my grandma talked to him, but I imagine she did. It wouldn't be for a while later that I had found out that prison would be his life. Later on, I believe he got out of prison, or jail, I don't really know which… all the same to me. He didn't stay free for long however. I don't recall when, but my grandma would later tell me that he was in prison again… for raping his 5 year old daughter. I never cared to ever see the man, and after that, knew that I didn't want to at all, ever again.

My mom, not too long ago seemingly, told me that one day, when I was ready, she would tell me the story of their time together and what he was like. They went their separate ways when I was only a year old or so. I've heard stories how loony he was, but I don't know how much of that story line is true, but I believe it wholeheartedly. One story involves him trying to gouge out his father's eyes with a spoon. He was a full-blown schizophrenic that, I guess, popped pills and probably took other drugs and stuff. I guess I'll wait until my mom decides to fill me in. I can probably do without hearing it though. I am sure that these memories aren't something she cares to think back on, either.

Life in Grade School

First Grade

I remember quite a bit from my early years in grade school. I remember my first and second-grade crushes. In first grade, the girl I liked peed herself in class. I would have died right there if it were me. I think she was too shy or embarrassed to ask the teacher if she could use the restroom. I remember the look on her face vividly: her eyebrows scrunched but elevated high on her forehead, the look of almost fear or shame in her eyes. I felt bad for her. And then it happened. A puddle formed on the floor and everyone in the class, except for me, pointed and laughed. I sat in the row next to her, so I got to talk to her a little bit. I think she liked me too. We gave each other our phone numbers, and I called her house one night after school and got to talk to her. Sadly, after the end of the year of first grade, she and her family moved away. I was saddened by this for a while, as I had been anticipating getting to see her again at the start of the new school year.

First grade, which is seemingly the equivalent of a high school education these days, was very good learning period to me. We learned to read and write like college students of today... See Bill. See Bill run. Run Bill run! We learned how to count and make change and how to tell time on those things with hands. I didn't discover digital until second grade. We learned a lot, but that was where recess ended for me.

Second Grade

In second grade, a few things happened to me. Other than my first-grade crush leaving the area, I found out what it was like to be left behind on Valentine's Day. My second grade Valentine's Day is the only one that I can vividly recall. I missed it.

It was a rainy day. Everyone had prepared boxes decorated with hearts and aluminum foil with slots on top for classmates to drop valentines in. Since it was raining that day, recess was held indoors. The classroom had a small plethora of board games and puzzles, and having never had the chance before to grab the game Connect Four, I was poised and ready to strike at it and gather it for myself. As soon as the bell rang, I sprung forth like a cheetah and seized my prey. In my victory dance, which only included spinning on the heels of my feet, I fell backward and caught the back of my head on a rectangular wooden table. I don't even know who I played the game with, after I got it though.

Once we were back in our seats for class, my second childhood crush informed me that I was bleeding… and that was the end of the day for me. I got taken to the principal's office to wait for my dad to pick me up from school. The following day, I got to enjoy a small bag of sweetheart candies and looked through a tiny pile of Valentine's cards by myself. Out of context, but the girl in the story for second grade; I recall being at recess and being dared to kiss her. Whether or not we did, I cannot remember. I could ask her if she remembers. I'm friends with her on Facebook.

Second grade didn't start with and end on Valentine's Day… sadly. And what happened in second grade didn't stay in second grade either - but it was kinda like Fight Club. At the beginning of the school year, a group of kids were picking on my younger cousin. At the time, he was too small to defend himself… and against the numbers, both of us would have been no match. I took it upon myself to rat on the students, in class… in front of everyone in the classroom… calling out names. This single action changed my life in school for the rest of my pre-college life. From that day forth, I was doomed to be picked on, harassed, and bullied to no end. There wasn't a corridor, room, locker, bus, anything, or anywhere that could separate me from that anxiety until I got home… and what awaited me there was not always pleasant. I will never completely lay blame on anyone for what has happened to me in my life, as I know I could have instigated a lot, but it wasn't as easy being me as it was to put a fake smile on my face and say, "everything's fine". Sadly, this is probably the 'norm' for so many people - especially back then, when discipline was a little more severe than a three minute timeout from your game console or phone.

Third Grade

Third grade rolled around. Recess was trouble. At that time though, being bullied never amounted to more than name-calling. It was bearable and I could still have some enjoyment. Getting to go down the metal slide… swinging bar to bar on the jungle gym and playing tag around the merry-go-round was still going on. I didn't anticipate how bad things would get for another year. I remember making a fool of myself though. I called my teacher "grandma" one day out of the blue, which she didn't mind, but I got a nice heckling for it.

Third grade was my first experience with death.

One day, after getting off the bus, my mom came up to me in the living room and said that she had something bad to tell me. Having never 'had' bad news before, I was excited. I had no idea. I've never had anything so bad in my life happen that it would be something that welcomed tears.

My mother had to gather the courage to tell me that my grandfather passed away, and as she did, tears started welling up in her eyes as she watched my heart sink. We had visited him a few times in the hospital. My grandmother would make up stories of his various conditions. One of my cousins and I were at the hospital, which would be the last time that we saw him. We played on the elevator for most of that visit. I'll never forget that, and I will never forgive myself, even if it was 'normal' for kids to play. When my mom told me what had happened, all I could do was cry. Nobody anywhere in my world would ever know where I was at that moment in time. At that age, I resented myself for how I spent my last moments with him. After all, he was like a father to me. Gone. Unfortunately, at the time, I only felt the loss one way. I had lost my grandpa. I didn't know what would happen later. As time went on, my visits with Grandma became less and less until I was no longer visiting with her. Only on rare occasions would I see her anymore after that.

Fourth Grade

Fourth grade came and went so fast, that I barely recognized it. I believe that that was the year that I fell asleep on the bus all scrunched up in a ball. The driver only looked under the seats to see if any legs were dangling, parked the bus, and disappeared. My mom found me a few hours after I hadn't arrived home from school. I also had another one of those excited moments. During a Spelling Bee practice in class, I spelled spaghetti "s, p, e, e, e, t, t, i". I knew how to spell it, but I was too excited to get a word that I knew how to spell, that I blurted out the wrong letters... almost as if I were stuttering.

I don't remember what year it really started, but I was spending more time with my grandma and uncle from my mom's side of the family.

My cousins, brother, and I would visit and go to bible school on Sunday with grandma and got to hang out with my uncle unless he had to work. I remember being there a lot. I live with my uncle now, and even though it's not the same house, he has a lot of the knick-knacks that were present in that old house that rekindle memories. I remember drawing cars and things and they'd stick them on the refrigerator. I made a little tiny flip book too. Fun times.

By this time, I had secured one friend from my class. He was a tall guy, towering over our first grade teacher by several feet... not saying much, because she was about the size as the rest of us when we were first graders. It was funny, because we all had our little children desks and he had a high school student desk in first grade. I spent a few nights at his house. His mom and dad were extremely nice to me. One year, they took us to Cedar Point, which at the time, for me, was the most wonderful thing that had ever seemingly happened to me. My priorities were bad... even back then. Within this friendship, grew my first addiction. We dipped snuff... Skoal, Copenhagen, things of that nature. This preceded any of my involvement with alcohol, but the sheer act of doing something and getting away with it without the parental figures knowing was a little bit of a rush.

I was also, around this time, hanging out with two kids a couple of miles down the road from our house. A brother and sister that I played with, an older sister... and their mom and dad. Their dad thought of me like a son, or so I have been told. I spent a great deal of time with them growing up. And, I had my third innocent kind of crush. As time went on, more and more kids seemed to gather around. We lived on a lonely country road outside of a town small enough to pee on if the wind was blowing. Most of the time, hide-and-seek was the game to play, but if there were enough of us, baseball and football got tossed in there. We spent a lot of time on bicycles. I wish I had that energy today.

Fourth grade ended and just like that, a chasm formed before my feet, showing me the gaping jowls of hell.

Fifth Grade

Fifth grade was a real bad experience all the way around. I'd already lost my grandfather, and this year would be the year that my mom had left my dad. I wouldn't see her for quite some time after she left. This was also around the time that I found out that the dad I lived with wasn't my biological dad. This was the year that my perception of what a family was supposed to be diminished to something resembling dog shit. I felt abandoned. My days were nothing but hell. I couldn't catch a break. If I wasn't being severely picked on at school, I was getting my ass spanked at home for stupid shit. That's how parents and even school staff operated back in those days. Every once in a while, the words 'you're not my real dad', would roar in my head and somehow that got me through a tough spot in my life. Instead of crying forever, I'd get mad, then get over it. I remember a few times on the playground being challenged to fight. One day in particular, a group of boys tried to get me to fight with someone who had been taking karate all his life. "He won't use his karate", is all that they'd tell me. Regardless, I was too chickenshit to fight anybody.

I think this was the first, and perhaps only year, where I got that assignment to write a phrase repeatedly for an entire recess. I had called one of my teachers 'Mr. Small Balls', which, I didn't have to do... his real last name was just as funny, I just didn't connect the dots at the time. So, I said that out on the playground, and some guys that didn't like me ratted me out. I wasn't the only one assigned to do some creative writing. Another kid was in there too, and he got the idea of writing the phrase only once, big enough to fill the entire page, front and back. Small Balls laughed when he handed it to him, and he let him off the hook. Unfortunately for me, I didn't get the same break... and I wasted a perfectly good piece of paper.

I began playing music in school band class. I was an expert at the recorder in third grade! I started out trying to play a flute. I was able to get it to squeak, but I couldn't produce real notes or play anything. I gave it a week. Once I decided that wasn't the instrument for me, I tried to get dad to let me play percussion! Nope. So, I settled for saxophone. I liked hearing people play it. I think the people that make it sound good use Auto Tune. I couldn't make it sound all sweet and sassy like that. So, that was my instrument until my junior year in high school. I switched over to trombone. Dad didn't like that instrument either. I was god-awful!

With my grandpa and mom gone, the remaining family was me, my stepdad, his mom, and my little brother. The only saving grace in that scenario is that that grandma could cook very well, and she kept the house clean – something that my brother and I would take over doing after she passed. That caused me more expected ass beatings. I complain a bit about being bullied now, but without understanding what I was doing, I was in turn bullying my younger brother. I tried to make him do dishes and other duties when it was my turn, and I would get mad when he ratted me out. He'd go to the phone hanging on the wall in the kitchen and as he'd dial the phone number, I'd click the hook to disconnect. This would repeat until I gave up. He'd make the call, and when dad got home, there was hell to pay.

Home life was calm compared to school now that I think about it. I knew what to expect at home. What was scary was not knowing what would happen once I got to school… every time the bell rang… before I got on the bus… while I was on the bus… Everything was scary until I got home because it was unpredictable. The funniest thing I remember doing though happened in one game of basketball in gym class. I somehow got the ball, wouldn't pass it, and ran to the wrong goal, tried my shot, and it bounced off of the backboard and rolled back down toward the other end of the court. That was my last time playing professional basketball. I was a bad ass!

All four of us: my two cousins, brother, and I, would do a lot of stupid shit outside. I remember one cousin capturing a frog and encasing it in mud and calling it Han Toad-o. My other cousin and I were sword fighting. I think I had a plastic tomato stake and he had one of our great grandfather's ceremonial military cutlasses. I got a little bit of a gash on my upper arm from the brutal battle that took place. I remember snakes being rampant... which here is where I'll tell you about the situation I was alluding to earlier on in the book. I didn't really have a super big fear of snakes out in the open. I didn't want to get bitten, but I wasn't necessarily afraid of their appearance. I DID have a fear of them creeping into my bed, which happened to take place around this time. My brother and I were going into the house, and I believe it was my brother that saw it first. A six foot black snake was climbing up into the top bunk of our bunk beds, which was my bunk! This will sound strange, but sometimes I feel as though shit that goes on in my head somehow predicts future events. It'll make more sense later.

At the end of the year, I told my dad that I wanted to switch schools. There were a few middle schools in our district. I thought that switching would change my life for the better. I rationalized with my dad, saying things like the other school would be closer to home. It worked. I started sixth grade at the new school.

Sixth Grade

But my troubles didn't end with the start of the new year.

Escaping the bullies I had from school up until the end of fifth grade was replaced with a lot more new bullies in sixth grade. One of them was even a relative! I believe that it was this year that I would experience death a second time, and in a sinister way, I was not only not sad, but

I could also have cared less. I didn't give a shit. He wasn't a friend of mine... but one of the bullies from all the way back in second grade - one of the ones that picked on my younger cousin. On the day of his funeral, a couple of friends and I were playing with toys in the classroom without having a care in the world. Giggling, laughing... having fun. One of my other bullies decided that I... not we... needed to be taught a lesson and he overturned my desk, with me in it, saying, "That was my friend!!!". Good for you, pal. I don't care. I didn't say anything. I just got up and went back to my desk. The only thing I remember after that was walking up to the funeral home around lunchtime. The person I did feel bad about was the person who shot him... the guy from fifth grade who knew karate and wouldn't use it on me if we fought. He is such a shit show now, from what I hear. He never escaped that hell... never amounted to more than the kid who shot his best friend in grade school by accident. If there is anyone in this world that I know, who has it worse than I ever did, it is that guy.

Living in our new house, to make matters worse, saw us all next door to a golf course. We had no business being on that, but that did NOT stop us. We were surrounded by wilderness. Many hundreds of acres of poison ivy, oak, and sumac... and access to 6 different towns... almost equidistant from each other if we went through the woods in the right direction. We didn't really cause chaos but we routinely drove our parents mad. I got blistered once, having to go tell my dad we were home from exploring the woods... on the other side of the planet. He snapped a switch from a tree and simply told me to run. I walked, not even hastening my pace, all the way to the house, repeatedly being struck on the ass. It hurt, a LOT, but I was not going to allow it to break me and take off running. After we got in the house, the switch got replaced with a belt. I got a few more spanks and then it was my brother's turn. It was hugely unfair, and the rule of law was, I was oldest and should have known better.

We build snow forts on the golf course greens. We'd use driving clubs on the greens, kicking up pieces of dirt and grass. We got to find out that those greens cost about $10,000 each to maintain. We took his boat out onto one of the ponds around the outside of one of the greens, in the woods. He drove down into the little cubby on a four-wheeler and sat there for about ten minutes before screaming, "Get the fuck out of there, right now!". We were hiding in the water on the other side of the boat. I think we thought that he'd believe that somehow, his little canoe just magically up-righted itself on the bank and slipped into the pond and floated to the middle of it. We got out. He spoke to our parents. I don't think we even got punished. I have no idea how he found out we were down there. I don't recall any people playing golf that would have seen us and notified him. I don't recall seeing anyone at all.

I haven't always been a major fan of snow, at least not before I began driving Jeep SUVs recently. But we don't get snow today like we did back then. We'd have ten foot tall snow drifts that the township would etch a sliver of road wide enough to squeak a bus through. We'd dig caves in them, sometimes one on top of another and play in them. We'd always be told we could end up buried in them. We didn't give a shit. One day, we got like six inches of snow overnight. The roads hadn't been plowed yet, and school, so far, was going to be on a two-hour delay. We all decided that we were going to go... HUNTING! I don't think any of us had ever fired a gun before, but how hard could it be? I grabbed the key to the gun cabinet off the top of it, cracked open the case and pulled out the coolest looking rifle there was. It was a .22 with a scope. We hunted cans. Any kind of cans that we could find in a little dumping area we had in the woods near a stream. Well, we probably each got a shot, missed all the cans, and returned to the house. I carefully put the gun away. We found out that school had not been canceled and ran up to the top of the hill to the road just in time to catch the bus on its way back from the end of the road. After school, after dad got home: Ass whoopin'. Somehow, we lost the rubber eye piece to the scope of the rifle while we were on safari. I don't know how he could spot this shit. If we were rough-housing in the place and a tiny crack got put into the wall, barely visible to us, he'd find it. Some things were a little more obvious... like a glass antique lamp that got brutally destroyed in our WWF heyday.

In sixth grade, we had a week-long camp with other neighboring schools - and there was gonna be a ho-down. We practiced square dancing all week the week before. It sucked. The following Monday, we all loaded up on the bus and headed for the woods. I think we went to Oglebay Park. We followed trails in the woods identifying trees and plants. We visited the zoo that they had, and got to check out an older than dirt house/building of some sort. I forget the name of it now. Then, the highlight of the trip came. They waited until it got dark, and in a lighted pavilion, it was time to dance! I, being awkward as I was and with very few friends, didn't have a partner to dance with right away. I had to be assigned to a partner. It was almost like an instant crush though. I got to dance with her briefly. She was from a different school, and I would soon be parted from her to not see her again until much later. When we did finally end up in the same school together, I found out she was on the slow side. I don't have anything against that, but, I wasn't going to pursue it, either. I don't think she may have talked to me more than once or twice, anyway.

This would be the first year that any kind of physical bullying actually took place. People were into arm wrestling and somehow, I ended up arm wrestling someone. We must have been pretty even, we couldn't move each other, but I held him upright for about 3 minutes with him popping veins in his face. We ended the little match and he was complaining his arm was sore. After class, I went into the restroom into a stall. He followed me in and tried to dunk my head in the toilet. I reversed it and put his face all the way down into the bowl, just shy of touching water, let him go, washed my hands and left. One less bully.

Seventh & Eighth Grade

Seventh grade came upon me like a whirlwind. I was now surrounded by every bully I had ever known… all in one place. It couldn't get much worse than that. There was nowhere to hide, no solace to be found, anywhere. By this time, I was getting to the point where I enjoyed the subject matter that I was learning in school, but at the same time, was surrounded by people everywhere that had it in for me from 8 am till 3 pm – Monday through Friday. The only safe place for me at the time was after I got off the school bus. Surprisingly, most of the kids that had a hard-on for me, didn't take the same buses that I rode, but that didn't deter those who were on the school bus I rode.

Between seventh and eighth grade, I was beginning to take note that more of the people that I could talk to that didn't want to kick my ass were female. My dad was with a new woman and her son had shown me how to play Rock You Like a Hurricane on guitar. I had, at this time, gained a few more friends and was beginning to take an interest in playing guitar more and more. I had been a band geek since fifth grade, playing mostly saxophone and later trombone and being in the marching band. I wish I had taken wood shop instead of home economics and band, though, for that was just another set of nails in my coffin. But I would rather surround myself with beautiful, talented women over smelly, brutal assholes any day.

Intro to Alcohol

I dare anyone to tell me that they themselves didn't or didn't know of anyone not of age, to at least once, consume alcohol if it was readily within reach. My friends down the road had daily access to all they could drink if they wanted it. After a while, we got bold. My brother and I would go visit and spend the night, nobody's parents the wiser. We would wait until their parents went to bed and grab some beer. Their dad had it on tap… which I thought was the coolest thing in the world. We couldn't handle too much… and it was more the thrill of having it than thinking about the consequences of drinking it. We were young and dumb, and yes… we had a lot of fun during those times. My brother and the brother of the two we were visiting didn't drink much, if any, but the sister, her friend, and I had no qualms about consuming adult beverages.

But in those times in my life, alcohol wasn't a problem. I didn't have cravings or withdrawals or anything. I didn't think about it at all if I wasn't holding one. Later, down the road, that would be a different story altogether, however. But, we weren't the only ones doing this. It seemed like most of the kids at school had their weekend stories and parties that I only ever got invited to once. I didn't go. I don't think I could have gotten my dad to say I could go, and I never asked.

We did some silly things. The sister and I would play hide-and-seek. I, being either stupid or being entirely too innocent, would hide with her. Oftentimes, we'd say we were pretending to be kissing so that her brother would find us and freak out. I never found out if that idea of hers was an invitation or just a prank. I'd go back today to find out if I could though. I feel that for most of my life, I have been driving with blinders on.

Her brother wouldn't drink. He wouldn't tell on us for doing it, but he swore to a life free of drugs and alcohol… at that moment in time. Later in his life, I believe he ended up the worst out of all of us though. My brother was a little friskier with alcohol later on in life, but not as much as I was, I don't think.

I would go back and relive these times if I could. Despite all of the sheer hatred being shown by bullies at school, and the ass beatings at home, this life right here, being with friends and my cousins was perhaps some of the best moments of my life - with obvious greater moment much later on in life.

Life in High School

Ninth Grade

Ninth grade introduced a few more douche bags to my not-so-friendly friends list. More bullies to make my life a living hell, one of which had to be in my favorite class. Drafting was one of the first classes that I had taken that had my full attention. I had a tiny bit of talent with doodling, but nothing as sophisticated as what I would learn in the courses I had with this teacher. The bully in the class is now the proud parent of a child who has been bullied. He doesn't like bullying now. Go figure.

English class became a lot more enjoyable as I was taking 'college prep' courses. Studying Shakespeare and the like, writing creatively using prose that has long left the school halls, made me feel like I lived on a different plane from the rest of the world. Little did I know that that kind of English would soon become a thing as archaic as the writings with which we learned. I don't remember the grades that I got in English, but I remember how involved the learning experience was.

I think that I might have started to get off of the bus on the way home from school to hang out with that tall-as-fuck dude. It might have been earlier than this though. I would hang out with him for a couple hours and then try to walk home (about 3 miles or so) before dad got home from work.

I also believe that my brother and I were also starting to visit with our mom. We'd go to visit her and her husband on weekends. Her husband had two kids of his own, slightly older than I was. They had a campground set up along a big creek with many others having similar setups. It was a bus with a wooden structure attached to it - all repurposed to provide a living space. We had a lot of fun out there. It's where my brother found his first crush that I knew about. He might have had others, but I am not privy to such information. He offered this girl cookies. Before presenting them to her, however, he had to make sure that he only gave her PERFECT cookies. There couldn't be broken-up pieces or crumbs. Only the finest would do. It was the cutest thing ever, and mom let him know this.

Most of the time, at the camp, we'd go play in the creek and either wade around near the camp site, or venture down further to a spot that was really deep where the creek bent in almost a ninety degree angle. We were always told to be careful there because there was an undercurrent that could pull us under. Eventually, my dad gave us an inner tube that we could use in the water. One day, I was inside it and saw a water snake coming straight toward me. I wasn't too startled, but I was cautious because I had heard that there were water moccasins in our area, and those are venomous. I just didn't know how to distinguish them.

There was also a Hare Krishna temple made of gold not very far away from the end of the road at the camp. When we finally got our bikes out to the camp, we'd ride up and down the road and finally found it and would check it out. It was crazy cool! I don't know anything about the people or religion, though. I never met anyone that belonged to that kind of group, and I never asked my mom or anyone what they might know about them.

There were two fights that took place while visiting with mom. One was on me. I was on this bridge of sorts made up of three long chains stretching between two structures of some large play set. I was about halfway across when some kids came up to where I was and started shaking the chains. I wasn't very high off the ground, but I got pissed off and told the guy that was doing it to fuck off, or something. He walked up to me and punched me in my face. I fell down, cried a bit and some other kid kept saying, "You shouldn't have fucked with him." I said some silly shit and then my brother and I went back to the house.

The second fight didn't result in any blows, but there was a bully giving my brother a hard time. I had a tiny pocketknife with me. We were standing on the outdoor basketball court. I took the pen knife out and held it out. I said, "Whoever gets it can use it," and tossed it up in the air and let it land on the ground. I was the one who picked it back up. My brother started crying, and once again, we went back to the house. I think that these two incidents happened very close to each other, perhaps only a few weeks apart.

Back in school, I didn't realize at the time that college prep courses were an escape route through my day. Ninety-nine percent of my league of bullies were not invited to participate. It didn't get rid of them entirely but left me at ease for much of my day.

Math was different. I took Trigonometry, Algebra I, Algebra II, Geometry, and Calculus in high school. Some of that stuff never made sense until rather recently, as I use some math in game development (for learning purposes only). I finally understand what sine and cosine are – 30 years after the fact. I don't think I did extremely well in those classes, but I know I didn't get below a C or so in any of them. I remember the hardest part of any of those classes was doing what is known as Proofs, either in Geometry or Trigonometry. I can't remember which. Calculus was wonderful. Even though I was too bashful to talk to a girl that I was 'seeing', we'd often pass notes before class. It was true love! The kind of love that makes modern romance novels look like... well... romance novels compared to what we had.

Biology was interesting. I was paired with a relative of my dad's (step-cousin? I don't know) and yet another girl that I had a small crush on. She dated a bully... We dissected a frog... I... dissected a frog – they took notes. It was quite fun once you got past the smell of formaldehyde. I remember that smell to this very day, and the sad thing is, once I became aware of what it smelled like and what it was used for, I realized that maybe, perhaps one of those little high-bounce balls that I played with HAD to have been made entirely of this substance.

As the number of bullies inflicting pain diminished, the number of friends that I had seemed to grow. Mostly, I wanted to hide during things like Phys Ed, lunch, and any normal classes. The rest of the time, I was met with kindness from a lot of people. I enjoyed school more and more, and had I known then that I would miss it someday, I would have held onto it a little more tightly. After graduating, it seemed like that life disappeared entirely.

One bully, who died later after graduation, found me in gym class one day. Earlier, I had doodled a person's head, and the nose was huge! I showed it to the wrong kid in class, saying that it was this other bully. So, in gym class, where I typically sat up in the bleachers rather than participate, he was already sitting up there. I didn't think anything of it, but he had some ill intentions for me. First, he asked me for some snuff. I gave him my can, he took some out, and then tossed my can all the way to the other side of the gym. He demanded that I go get it, and I refused. I was sitting with him sitting behind me. I just watched the other kids playing something. All of a sudden, he puts me in a choke hold. It hurt; I couldn't breathe and couldn't think of any way to get out of it. He held on for a good bit and then let go. After that, he was calling me names in a sinister tone. Finally, the period was about to end. It was time to go to the locker room and change - which I didn't have to do. I got up and started to make my way across the floor to leave. He came running behind me. I didn't think fast enough, and he tackled me. He didn't punch me. He could have. I got up and just continued walking. I believe that right after that, he never did anything to me again.

There were some other, not-so-violent bullying still going on, but one day, I think he might be a relative… came up on me and was trying to pull and toss me around… and couldn't. I grabbed him by the arm and, like the Hulk-a-maniac, spun him around me and slung him down the hallway. I got caught by a teacher, and he and I ended up with a three-day in-school suspension. This is where I learned a good lifelong lesson. The only time a person gets caught doing something bad is when that person is YOU doing something you shouldn't. Seemingly, everyone else gets away with murder.

Tenth Grade

Tenth grade wasn't very different from ninth grade, other than the classes I was taking. I was taking Drafting 2, which was still very cool. I drew an awesome device called a bone crusher. It utilized what is referred to as a rack and pinion - similar to what older style cars used for steering. We used Mylar drawing paper, which is more of a plastic than a paper. Then, we used airbrushes and colored construction paper to make the drawings pop! It was the most fun I had had in any class up to that point. The bully who no longer likes bullies was still there. He told me that he fucked my mom one day. I told him that my mom was dead with a hint of a sneer in my voice. He got all somber and apologetic… then I told him I was lying. The bullying immediately returned to normal the next day. He got what was coming to him, though. He pissed off the wrong dude, which happened to be another one of those step-cousins of mine. He got his ass CLOCKED. Good job, step-cousin!

We had an open lunch at this school. We could go uptown to the store and hang out there for lunch. Not always, but occasionally, a teacher may come up the sidewalk, but for the most part, we were completely unsupervised. It was during this time that I went from always just rubbing snuff to smoking cigarettes. All it took was one female to tell me that snuff was gross and that I should smoke instead. Hell with peer pressure, all someone had to say was, "Hi". What's crazy is that I could be flirty there, but not with the woman I would be with until shortly after graduation. Most of the time, I was a quiet, shy thing that people acted astonished if I said anything that could even be perceived as perverted.

I am not a racist, but this might come off sounding like I am. There was a new kid in the school - a black dude. He seemed to hate a lot of people, but not as much as me, and at first, he didn't have any reason to. I don't know what started the little spree that I had, but I would go to the office in between classes and claim items from the lost and found. I don't know what prompted it and am not sure why I thought I could get away with it. I only did it twice because the second time I did it, the person that owned the item saw me in class wearing it. It was a dingy blue jacket. He came up to me and said it was his. I told him, "No, it's mine." Not to be like, it is mine, now... I just pretended that it was always mine. He proved it was his, though, when he told me to pull the candy out of a specific pocket. So, after doing that, we were mortal enemies for about two weeks. He'd tease me and call me fucked up names. One day, we're in the library. He's sitting with about four or five other goons, and they are all talking shit non-stop at me. After the bell rang and we were out in the hall, he thought he'd get a little rough with me. I picked him up off the ground and slammed his ass into a locker. No more bullying from at least one more person for the rest of my days. Three down, a hundred to go.

Eleventh & Twelfth Grade

My Junior and Senior years were different than most of my lower grades. We had a new school built in our district that would house all of the high schools that were previously scattered around. So many students that I had never met before. Some nice... some not. It was a cool building. It's fancier than anything I went to previously. I made more friends, but now, it seemed as though one-third of the population was out to get me. Up until graduation, that would be the ongoing story of my life. From the instant I stepped into second grade until I tossed my graduation cap, day in and day out, I was bullied. And I know I wasn't the only one. I wouldn't grow a backbone until much, much later in life... and thankfully, so far, having a backbone doesn't mean there is a trail of bodies all over the ground somewhere.

Somewhere in this mess, I experienced another death. She was one of my favorite bus drivers. She was the very best! Too kind to have had to go so far before her time. She kept us in line, but at the same time, knew that kids were kids, and she let us smoke or rub snuff... as long as we kept it clean. Hell, sometimes, we'd even take the extra step to pick up a broom or some paper towels and Windex to help clean the bus on our way home. Nobody ratted on anyone... and to this day, I believe that the only people who knew that it took place were the kids on the bus. She'd have us wait until there were only a few of us who did such things remaining on the bus. I could get away with dipping snuff, but for those that smoked, that only took place after enough kids were off the bus for the day. She had a lot of love and respect from the kids she drove from house to house. I don't think I ever met someone who had such a loving heart for kids that they didn't know too well. She was a welcomed breath of fresh air, especially after a day full of dread.

I think it might have become a thing when we started hearing the song, "Smokin' In the Boy's Room", because starting in my Junior year, people were doing it. I don't remember noticing it happening too often until we got to the new school. Teachers would take turns around every fifteen minutes going into the restrooms to try to catch people lighting up. I went back to dipping snuff because it was easier to hide. It was less waste too. Firing up a smoke, taking a few puffs, and then dropping it into a toilet just wasn't very cost-effective.

Once I graduated and got my license, I worked for about a year before going to college. For $4/hr, I was one of the helping hands for an old, retired funeral director. I think you can think of the job as something like Hospice care. I had evening duties. I made sure he was fed, bathed, and took his medicines, but other than driving him to church, meeting friends and family, and going to restaurants, we spent a great deal of time either in his office or out on the porch and smoked. Sometimes, he would offer me a cigar, and we'd just sit and wave at people as they drove by. For that insignificant amount of money, the job was downright nasty. I wouldn't go back to doing that for $40/hr.

During that time, I spent a great deal of time with one of my best friends, playing guitar. If I wasn't driving to his house, he would come over to mine, after he got his car running, that is. I miss that guy a lot. After returning home from almost ten years outside of the area, I found out that he had died while I was away. I rarely came home to visit. I never got to say goodbye. We had a shared friend, who owned a guitar… would hold the guitar… and to this day, the only person I knew that could snap a low E string and just giggle like a fool. We had a ton of fun! So sad that it was short-lived. I don't know what ever became of Bottom E… he faded into the distance like a dream you wake up from and can't remember.

I had another death shortly after I had moved back home - my grandmother on my biological father's side. Another "goodbye" that never got spoken. I remember wanting to go to her funeral and not being able to. I remember taking time off work because of it. I remember my dad telling me that I used her death as an excuse to take off work. I remember that being the first time I ever said, "FUCK YOU!" with the most amount of raw anger I had ever felt in my life. That woman hopefully had felt the amount of love I held for her. I look back and think of myself as an asshole forever driving past her house without stopping. Something I did frequently, as I had a paper route for a while that went right past her house. I regret it now.

As a Lover – Part 1

In High school

I can't remember when exactly it took place, but I know we were a thing for quite some time. For the first time, I would not only declare to have an interest in a girl but also get to date the person of interest! And I blew it. I was too shy to talk to her most of the time. We sometimes passed each other notes, but other than going to proms and homecomings, we spent very little time together.

I didn't get to start driving until after I graduated high school. Other than the dances we attended, and before I could drive, I had gone to visit her only once. My brother and I rode our bikes down the long hill into a small conglomerate of towns near her. While we were down there, I thought it would be a cool idea to go see her. We spent a whole fifteen minutes, it seemed, and were on our way to climb the hill we easily coasted down not too long before. As much as I liked her, and my feelings of wanting to stay, I felt embarrassed with my brother standing next to me while we were there.

Even though I couldn't express it, I liked her. I liked being with her. When someone spoke ill of her, I took offense, personally. It doesn't seem as though age matters, or at least back then, it didn't. If you had a name that easily rhymed with something... there was at least one kid that would utter it... repeatedly. My dad's name, my last name, her last name... somewhere, at some point, was used in a sentence with other words that sounded like them. It pissed me off – to no end.

We went to every dance. We didn't miss a single one. Sadly, that was the highlight of our entirety together. She came to my graduation party. My friends and I played guitar and hung out with each other, while sadly, she stood there by herself feeling awkward among people she didn't even know. Looking back, I feel like a total ass, but at the time, didn't know how to act at all... especially as a boyfriend.

I took her out to eat once and to the movies a few times after I got my license, which she got tired of quickly. I didn't know what she was expecting until 'that' hit me. I knew what was wrong, once it was too late. I visited her once while she was in college. It was her and I alone in the room all night. Her roommate kind of giggled toward us, thinking something sly was about to go down. I slept on the floor, and she in her bed. We didn't even do as much as kiss the entire time. I did try to impress her by driving fast on the freeway. I don't think the effect took hold.

I only remember kissing her one time that didn't involve her right cheek. If it wasn't the only time, it was the first and only time that it was done passionately. It was a goodnight kiss, after which she whispered, "Call me.", which I never did – very regrettably.

Looking back, I think that my entire life post-high school would have been so much better than what it ended up being. I honestly believe that I would have strived to become instantly better than what I have taken a lifetime to accomplish – only to have failed miserably. We met up once more a few years later. I took her to the movies. When I dropped her off afterward, she told me, "If I ever need a ride to the mall again, I'll call you.". That wasn't the last time I ever spoke to her, but I made sure that the next time would be, several years later when she tried to contact me to tell me how wonderful her life was. I was drunk when

I told her to fuck off. I don't regret it… well… maybe I do, a little bit. She told me that she was sorry that I turned out to be an asshole and disappeared. At the time, I assumed that I was NOT an asshole. History has proven otherwise.

After High School

I wouldn't come into a feeling of love for a very long time after my high school sweetheart days. Up until that point, I had thoughts of what sex would be like, but never experienced it. A couple of my friends, my brother and I went to visit a girl after I was out of school. She played bass guitar, and it was her birthday. Before this day, we never hung out together. I had the idea that it would be fun to go with our guitars and all hang out. She had other things in mind, and I think everyone else was in on it. I kind of ended up being the birthday cake, I guess. From innocent shy guy to BOOM!… Okay! Game-changing, mind-altering fun with someone that I didn't know, had no intentions with doing anything like that with… and well… it didn't last very long. We hung out for about two or three months, and that was it. I took her to a concert. People that we passed would talk shit… made me angry, but we just kept walking. Later on, another step-cousin was walking with her in front of me and they looked at me and called me stuck-up. I guess I was. I didn't think so.

This became more of a norm than I ever imagined for a long time. Long periods of loneliness accompanied by sparse bursts of 'Hello there, little one!'. I can't say that I didn't have fun in those moments, but it was hardly anything that I was dreaming about having. One woman would shake the apples out of my tree, but that too faded quickly. I would see her again for almost a year before the whole deal blew up in my face. I don't know what she wanted from me, but it wasn't my undying affection. I don't remember when it started, but she had me writing poetry. Either way… love, hate, cuddly, or disgustedly… I was writing poetry. I still have most of it. This love story wouldn't take place for quite some time, however.

Life in College – Part 1

I thought I was ready. I thought I was intelligent enough. I had all the wheels engaged in four-wheel drive. And it didn't take long for me to figure out that drinking and driving wasn't a good mix. Literally and figuratively. Figuratively for now.

I had an enormously huge idea, that happened in a dream… of how to propel vehicles into space using magnetism. The idea would be akin to bullet trains – and something that someone somewhere now is proposing. An idea like that convinced everyone including my dad that I was prepared to do great things in life. It didn't take long for me to let everyone, including myself, down.

I am not sure why I chose the field that I went for. I wasn't, in any way, into technology, but I chose to go to school for electronics engineering. The only experiences I had with technology were a short stint inside of one of my mom's college text books on Basic, playing video games, and a dream on how to launch a rocket by seemingly unrealistic means at the time.

On day one of moving into my residence for college away from home, I am welcomed into the 'brotherhood' with a big fat forty-ounce beer. Not being a stranger to beer, I gladly accepted it. The bigger of the two dudes that got it for me thought it hilarious to see me chug it all in one go and then pass out on my newfound bed. It was hilarious enough for them to make it a daily ritual. Before long, it was indeed a daily ritual spanning decades.

Classes began. At first, I was going strong. I did well. The school I was attending had trimesters rather than semesters. I got through the first two most honorably. But by the middle of the third, I started falling behind, fast. I was spending a great deal of time playing video games, and by that time, drinking more than just one big beer. I was working a part-time job on the side as well, so I wasn't spending very much time, if any, studying and doing homework. Shortly, I wasn't going to my morning classes, then morning and afternoon.

Soon, I wasn't going to class at all. A few weeks went by before getting a notice to talk to people at the college. I went in and was told about my current situation, that I was falling behind severely, but that all my professors had agreed that I could get back into the swing of things with a grade of C in each course if I were to resume courses immediately.

I went back to classes... briefly. I was dumbfounded in every single topic – which would have to be expected. If I were to take the matters into account seriously, I would have to study non-stop just to catch up and hope to pass each course by the end of the trimester.

I did not take advantage of what was offered to me. I may have gone to classes another day or two and ended up skipping once more.

At this point, I was on the border of losing my job. The car I had... the first car I had that I loved, broke down on me one night on my way home from work. It was around 2 or 3 am, and I just happened to break down in the very worst neighborhood a person of my caliber should break down in. Not knowing what I found out almost instantaneously once I knocked on the first door to a house with lights on, I tried to get some help. I don't remember how my roommate ended up being there, but he was there when I knocked on the door. The guy was huge, and was as shocked as I was, that I was there, in that neighborhood, at that time of night, and not full of holes... his words, not mine. I looked at my roommate and asked him, rather seriously, "Do you know this guy?". I am not sure if the guy at the door thought I was the very least threatening individual on the planet or what, but he let me come in and use the phone to call for a tow truck. I had only ever smoked weed once in my life. I knew the smell though... and so did probably everyone in this neighborhood if this guy opened his windows. There were women bouncing around half-naked, enough smoke to probably put the neighborhood in a panic with firetrucks rolling down the street... and now, the deadly thought that I should NOT be here running through my mind.

My car got towed. I am not sure how it made it all the way back to my dad's house back home. He had it for a short time, and when he told me that it was 'running' again... against his best intentions of not wanting me to spring back into the driver seat until it was thoroughly tested out... I drove it and it blew up a few days later.

I lost my job.

My next vehicle was a blue pickup. It was a mess. If you opened the hood with the engine running, you could see liquids of various colors spewing out of it all over the place. It was a laughingstock. Well, the big guy that my roommate had as a friend took a joyride with me one night after a bit of drinking. The truck had a loud exhaust, and of course, I had to show off and go speeding down a side street with it. Well, I called the attention of a police officer to myself who followed me to my complex. He asked me what we were doing and whether we had been drinking. I am not sure how I reworked the conversation into my being a student at the college, but he said that his son also went there. He told us to have a nice, SAFE, evening, and drove off. That could have been my very first DUI.

The school invites me to talk to the same people again. I got a well-deserved speech about how I was wasting their time and my money... ended up $15,000 in debt and didn't know what to do.

A Degree in Alcohol & Game Testing

I make fun of my life back then. I often tell people that when I started my college career, I majored in Alcohol and minored in Gaming. It's not entirely funny, but what else can I do about it now? I didn't stop drinking, even after realizing that it just ruined my fresh step into the world. My life became a party… for a very long time. I didn't give a rat's ass about anything other than what new video game was coming out and who was going to hand me my next beer, because where I was heading, I didn't make enough money to fund my own drinking problem.

Every single day was a party, and we partied even harder on the weekends, because… well… it's the weekend! Let's live it up! From playing Dungeons and Dragons, Poker, PlayStation, and placing bets on NASCAR, every minute of life equated to an ounce of beer. From my early twenties, 9 PM became the most opportune time to take a nap, simply because alcohol said so. After I got a bit of tolerance built up, I'd often stay up until the wee hours of the morning only to get a few hours of sleep before dizzily waking up to take a shower before work. At one workplace, I was greeted every morning by a guy who said, "Looks like you had a rough night!". I didn't have a rough night; I was simply doing the same old thing with new people finding out about it at that point.

I had a habit of drinking to the point where I'd pass out. Something that I didn't really think about was the fact that I wasn't brushing my teeth before bed. Often, I would be vomiting at some people before I did make it to bed. With all the sugar in the beer, the acid in the vomit, and not brushing like I should, I'd come to have a little problem later that I will be talking about.

When you go see a doctor today, they ask you if you drink, smoke, do drugs, etc. When you tell them that you do any of those things, they will tell you that those things are bad for you. I never really ask, but I wonder if people that tell you these things believe that you have no idea what you're doing. I KNOW they are bad for me. I didn't just enter the world a few seconds before lighting that cigarette or grabbing that beer right before you showed up!

It's easy to fall hard when you are in constant contact with others who do bad things. I've been told once, "You are only as successful as the people you surround yourself with". I believe that 100 percent. I wouldn't realize that until much later, but by the time I found it out for myself, it was half past too late.

Life in the Workplace – Part 1

If I knew where my life would ultimately take me, I would have done everything I could have done to keep that job that I had lost while attempting to ruin myself in college.

Pizza Person – Part 1

With the help of a couple friends that I made during my brief stay at school, I got introduced to the pizza career. I was hired as a cook making $6.00/hr. I was lucky that I knew people that I could end up living with during my entire lifetime away from my hometown, because, at $6.00/hr., I couldn't afford to pay rent and utilities on my own. I maintained this status for quite a while. From the time I left home, until after I came back, days, months, years… they all seem to have happened instantaneously. Before I knew it, college was a thing long gone… as long gone as my brain… as by that time, I was drunk more than I was sober.

With the loss of my beautiful car, I went through a few other vehicles, but one belonged to my brother. It could have been fixed up and been an awesome truck, but I got a hold of it – and like so many things, messed it up eventually. While I had it, the engine in it also blew up. My brother, only 15 years old at the time, came up and swapped the engine in a single day. I had found a replacement engine for it – truck and all for $150. We rented an engine hoist and in the parking lot of my apartment complex, performed a somewhat successful transplant. The engine was put into place, and we knew the engine could run, but when my brother put the distributor cap on, it was out of phase 180 degrees. It wouldn't start. It took a little bit of time to figure out the problem, but before he left, the truck was on the road. It didn't have a heater core, so… the upcoming winter would prove it to be a little less than satisfactory. With the spare truck, I was able to snag a bunch of interior pieces that were missing out mine: vent covers, knobs, etc.

Eventually, I got bumped up to being a shift manager. I got a pay raise. I was up to $6.50/hr. I was the least capable person on the planet to get other people to do what I told them to do, but I kept that hat for like five years. I never got more than a nickel or dime raise per year. I could have done without the upgrade to glorified cook. it wouldn't have made a single difference. Either way you slice it, I was a broke assed bitch.

Being a shift manager meant that you would either open the store and get it ready for business, or close up shop, clean up, and prepare the deposit to be taken to the bank in the morning.

It was a Friday night. It was cold out with snow on the ground. My truck was out in the parking lot with heavily frosted windows. I had driven it home, somehow, in similar circumstances before… I just never got caught doing it - until that night. The time or so that I had pulled this stunt before, the windows would thaw out enough to see what was in front of me from the heat of the engine.

It was 3 am or after, and I had tried my best to warm the vehicle to get the frost to thaw, but it just wasn't happening. I decided that I would just go ahead and drive it. I wasn't drunk or drinking, but I was stupid enough to think it would be 'fine'.

I got to the very first red light from the shop… which was right in front of the store. I waited for the light to turn green. I couldn't see past the windshield, and I didn't think to just drive with my head sticking out of the window. I was literally driving blind. Well, luckily, I didn't have to go far. Home was far away, but I didn't get more than 50 feet from the red light before being flagged down by a flashlight held by an officer up ahead of me.

A severe accident closed the road, which was four lanes wide, going both ways. If it weren't for the officer flagging me over, I would have driven right into it.

He thought that I had been drinking. He ordered me to turn off the engine – still in the right-hand lane of the street, rather than off to the side of the road. I was asked to recite the alphabet. I finished, without singing "Now I know my ABCs…", and he asked if that was all of it. Not even 2 minutes later, I am rear-ended by a woman coming from a bar across the street from the shop at 45 miles per hour. All it did was fold the bumper of my truck under the bed, but it totaled the front end of her car.

Suddenly, the question of my sobriety flew out the window, and the two of us found ourselves in the back seat of the officer's cruiser exchanging insurance information. I could smell the alcohol emanating from her, but obviously the officer didn't. I didn't say anything. I waited for my roommate to come get me and went to get my truck the following morning.

I think I could have done something if I had taken down the officer's badge number, but upon careful consideration, I believe I would have done more harm than good for myself by starting something.

Happened to be that the girl that rear-ended me gave false information. She didn't have coverage, and the address she gave while we were in that back seat together was fictitious as well – or it was an old address. Somehow, I was able to look her up on the internet and found her phone number. I called her and she was like, "Oh yeah…".

An insurance adjuster came to look at the truck and totaled it out.

Before all of this, I spent money to get a spiffy intake, carburetor, and air filter cover for it. Edelbrock.

I ended up selling the truck to one of my newer roommates who needed something for work. He was in construction. He took off all the fancy garments, including the hood that had a scoop on it. He didn't want anything that would draw attention to himself. I think he sold the parts for pocket money. I never thought to call my brother to see if he wanted it back. Turns out, years later, the original owner (a stepbrother) inquired about it. I told him it was wrecked and left it at that.

I made friends with a lot of people. I had fun with a lot of people. I was the person with the party going on every day after work. One of my roommates didn't mind, but some did during my days of hardcore partying.

I was now only associating with other people who partied. I am very lucky that my indulgence stayed within the confines of alcohol, because some of my friends back then were not that lucky. One is a recovering crack addict. And one, I am not sure where her head is at anymore.

My first roommate, the one that kind of kick-started my drinking career, was a roommate of mine for a long time. He and the two friends that got me into pizza… we all kind of drifted through life together. The first roommate… took a job packing trucks, much like I did, but for a different outfit, and left school because that job was going very well for him. Later, he would move away and try to maintain his distance as he needed to escape the bad, unhealthy habits that we were enjoying. Not soon after he moved on, he had a stroke. I haven't heard from him since.

The manager of the store was a woman with five children, and slightly above average good-looking for someone her age. I can say that now… now that I am older than she was back then. Eventually, the employer-employee relationship became more like friendship. She would go to a bar with some of us. We'd gone to a concert together… her and a few of us from work. She told us that she would be flashing her boobs if we weren't there. Devastated me!!! My meager wage no longer seemed to be the glue that kept me there for as long as I stayed there.

Sooner or later though, I knew that I needed to do something better.

First Computer-Related Opportunity

By this time, I had my little gathering of friends, some in pizza, and some from school. I had been taking on more interest in computers at that time other than just gaming. I was getting familiar with HTML, CSS, and JavaScript. I was building my very own website and my own machines! I thought it was the coolest thing in the world (I'm noticing I say this a lot... apparently, a lot of things were the coolest thing in the world ever!) The website was cheesy, and even today, when I build something I have complete control over, my skills in making something pretty... are lacking. I just throw opacity variations of colors everywhere. But I was learning. I had a good amount of knowledge of software tools and operating systems. A friend started talking about how I had taught him everything he knows about computers and told me that he would put in a good word for me where he worked. I immediately drew up a resume, handed it to him, and was quickly interviewed for a logistics position with the company with the opportunity to propel myself into hardware break-fix.

Logistics was a far cry from what I wanted to do, but at least it was a nice step up in the right direction. Once again, I felt that my life might start going in the right direction. Years of torment (not so much) of working at a pizza place had finally turned into an opportunity to do something more fulfilling for a whopping $10/hr.

This is where I met the girl that I said shook the apples from my tree. She was married when she first started. I was instantly attracted to her though. I would go out of my way to do 'good deeds' for her 'out of the kindness of my heart'. I even created a little website for her centered around a favorite anime of hers. She is the person that got me into anime.

Not very long after meeting her, maybe two or three months, she would come to visit me at my apartment, and a short-lived thing happened. She came by a few times. I took her to dinner once. She spent the night a few times. Suddenly though, she disappeared without warning, and I wouldn't see her until years later. I knew that she was going through a divorce at that time. Nobody at work knew about it. They assumed she was happily married. She told me differently.

When she disappeared, my roommates and one of their girlfriends were telling me that she wasn't worth the sadness I was feeling. They wouldn't tell me why. I had to figure it out on my own. Eventually, I found out that she was a druggy. I didn't know what she was into, just that she had done stuff, without me knowing, with some of my friends. Much later, I found out that she was into crack cocaine.

Shortly after getting into this new workplace, the manager who hired me (who I liked a lot) got replaced by a younger guy (whom I didn't like a lot). Every chance he got, he looked down at me, as if he were a supreme being of some sort. I couldn't do anything right, but by that time, I had moved on from Logistics and was working out in the field. At $10/hr., he assumed that I should be living the dream and dressing the part. He would put me down or look at me funny. I don't know why. I do know that by this time, with my drinking, it was more apparent to more people than not, that I had a problem.

I think I was on my fourth or fifth vehicle since my pride and joy blew up. I was now driving a Cadillac with a moon roof that I had to wedge shut with a 2" x 4". It was the most comfortable car I have ever owned; I just didn't care to be seen driving it.

I felt insignificant in the field. I didn't understand as much as I thought I did, but I was bound and determined to make it last because I never wanted to go back to working in food.

I ended up, for about six months, at one facility doing upgrades and installations. It was the first and only time I had ever been in a facility that was operated by both union and non-union staff. When there was a strike, we were told not to come to work for safety reasons. The extreme difference between the union and non-union parts of the building were night and day. The union parts were sparkly clean and the parts that weren't were reminiscent of a train yard filled with graffiti-covered railway cars. I wouldn't necessarily classify the difference between the two types of employees as clean vs dirty or intelligent vs stupid, but it was evident that there were those working there that gave absolutely no fucks about where they worked or what they did - no respect for having a job at all. If they knew what I know now, you would be able to walk through the entire building and not be able to tell that there was a division between work types.

While there, we had an assignment to go to a city and install a Windows work group. We had to set up a few servers and a bunch of workstations. It was fun!

The work assignment that we had was extremely simplified thanks to the one guy out of the group of us with like a Master's Degree in the Space/Time Continuum. He concocted a script that would run the entire process for each machine. Only one of the five of us need be present to execute the batch file and it was off to the races. I think I only had to be there once for a few minutes and that was it.

The lead tech and I, being the heavier drinkers than the rest of the group, decided to go out for drinks. We ended up at the sleaziest dive bar the city had to offer. He had a thing for Wild Turkey, while I was still just a beer drinker, but I drank whiskey that night with him, following each shot of Turkey with a beer or two. I know I was at that 'happy' drunk point when I noticed her, but he was thoroughly wasted.

There was a girl at that bar in the far-back corner all by herself. She was very beautiful, at least at my level of impairment at the time. No, she was indeed beautiful. She was about to leave, and as she was about to walk past, I coerced her to come drink with us for a bit. She gladly accepted.

We drank for a while, then she excused herself for a moment to go to the restroom. As she was returning, she touched her hair, and I could have sworn that her full head of hair moved. When she got to us, I inquired about it. Her response was a total removal of a wig. Underneath were strands and patches of hair, half shaved, half dangling.

I didn't know what to say. I tried to be silly, and unintentionally ended up insulting her, I think. She was there drowning in sorrow trying to mentally prepare herself for a work meeting the next morning, and I, in stupidity, said something offensive. She excused herself, left the bar, and soon after, so did we. Before any of us left, the other guy was trying to convince her that I was a nice guy: a guy that she should consider hanging out with after we all left the bar. At the time, even I would have believed him. I thought I was.

The offensive thing that I said was, "Know what would be cool? If you dyed all those splotches of hair different colors!". Today, that idea would have been normal, if not already implemented. Back then, it would have been downright revolutionary… at least in my drunkard way of thinking. It's not the first time or the last time that I would say something stupid.

It was around this time, I found out that my whole life of being an introvert had taken a turn for the worse. I don't believe that I have ever said something so offensive, insulting, degrading, or stupid to another human being in all my life. To this day, it is probably the worst thing I've ever said to anyone.

The other guy… couldn't walk straight. When I say couldn't walk straight, he took up the entire street while he walked down it. If you ever witnessed how an eel or snake swims in the water, that was this guy! He was too drunk to remember where our hotel was. I didn't pay attention to how we got there. Navigation was limited to the one or two times I played Pin the Tail on the Donkey – only, we were two tails and a whole ass with no sense of direction.

I saw a homeless man slumped over against the side of a building on the sidewalk. Out of desperation, I asked him, "Where is the Crown Royal", to which... he produced his half-empty bottle in a kind gesture toward me to have a sip. I was referring to the name of the hotel where we were staying. I didn't take a sip from the bottle. What do you think I am, an alcoholic?

I had one more assignment with the company before I was let go. It was a government establishment. Engineers would draft military designs of all kinds and then store and print them. I was in a group of 3 people designated to maintain the equipment, mostly the 3-part printers that the engineers used.

These printers were enormous... about the size of a full-sized refrigerator put on its side. The processes included dot-matrix, a laser/chemical process that etched the schematics onto a tiny plastic window, and a punch process.

I remember sleeping off the previous night's drunk most of the time I was there, only to be awakened when it was time to clean. Another enormous monstrosity taking up space in the building we were in was the server. The server was a room filled with electronics. The storage system was another box bigger than a refrigerator that contained 16 1 gigabyte platters larger than a laser disc, and each about half an inch thick. It was the type of machine that you'd expect in a sci-fi movie. Shortly before I would be escorted out of the building, losing my job, they replaced that huge room and 6 of those very complex and large printers with a little Dell desktop computer and a CD burner that operated itself with a little robot arm and 3 spindles to hold the CDs before and after print.

I had a nice three-year fling with opportunity before it fell back in on itself. The company had been bought out and then dissolved.

Pizza Person – Part 2

After my little jaunt in the business world, I found myself back in the pizza gig. I went back to work for the same manager I had previously, only in a new location. It was a nice neighborhood – a dry town. Crime was basically unheard of there.

Not being too bright, I would have drivers buy my beer slightly right before closing time at stores outside of the area... sometimes ending up with no beer. I never used my head and bought my beer before work – even though I worked the evening shift and had plenty of time to do so beforehand.

A lot of the same people still worked for this manager, and once again, being a shift manager (glorified cook), I had no control over them. I would end up being one of the few people who did any of the necessary work before we left for the night. Only other people responsible for closing the store did any of the dishes or prep for the next day, and somehow, I oversaw doing more of the upper management duties than I was supposed to have.

It was still a party environment though. Even though the new store was further away, the nightly (early morning) parties continued.

I would eventually leave this place, only to work briefly for another pizza place for a small period before a major life-altering event took place.

Alcohol – The Downward Spiral - Part 1

I tried not to do it very often, but it did occur that I would drive after indulging on a few adult beverages. I had been pulled over a few times but never got a DUI.

One day, on a day off from work, I had to work on my car. For a few nights before fixing the car, I would drive it and the battery would die and the engine would overheat – seemingly in unison. It ended up being the alternator belt – it had stretched to a point where it wasn't providing enough tension for the alternator to recharge the battery or crank the water pump enough to avoid the engine from overheating.

I was working on my car still when I received a page from work. I went inside, like a dumb ass, and called. I was told that the person that would oversee closing the store had called off and that I HAD to come in to work. I explained that 1: I had been drinking, and that 2: I was working on my car and that it was not in an operational state. I was told that I had to get there immediately after fixing my car, or I would be fired. I was drunk… not buzzed, when I got the car running. I put on my clothes and headed in to work. I didn't think that losing that job would have been perfectly fine by me, but I knew that I was already living in poverty and any break in income would not go well.

I was on the highway (outer belt of Columbus, OH). I was familiar with my path to work but managed to pull off on the wrong exit. Unable to get back onto the highway because I was too drunk to realize that the on-ramp would be in the opposite direction I was now heading, I was cruising down the street – a 4-lane road. A car full of people wanting to exit a strip mall pulled out into the 2 lanes that I could take and stopped dead, blocking both. I was going too fast and didn't have enough distance to come to a complete stop before striking their vehicle. I had reduced my speed enough to only induce tiny damage to their vehicle, but it prompted a call to 911 which led to the police arriving at the scene. An officer questioned me about my speed, which I thought was the speed limit. He said that he could break out a tool that would tell him exactly how fast I was going. I feared only a speeding ticket.

The incident led to all of us being piled into the police officer's car, where more questions took place and the sharing of insurance information. Before leaving the vehicle with simply a ticket, the driver of the other car, in a street-slang-filled voice exclaimed that she smelled alcohol. I was taken down to the station, put in a cell, charged with my first DUI, and got to place my only phone call. I called my pizza place, asked for someone to come get me out… and had to go to work… trashed. Immediately entering the place, I made my way to the nearest trash can and threw up. I don't think we even cleaned the store after closing.

My court date was coming up. The night before, there was a concert that I attended. It was an Ozz-Fest concert. I had a nice drunken time, which culminated in a few sexy encounters. There was a group of three girls behind me. One of them was incredibly attractive, and eventually, knowing that I was interested in her, her friends deprived her of all her clothes except for her bra and panties. I inquired what she planned to do after the show, but nothing happened. I went home… the girl that I was engaged in adult activities at the time was there waiting for me. We had sex, she left in the morning before I woke up, and I had arrived late, without a phone call, to my court hearing. I was blasted on – being told that I am lucky I wasn't going to be put into jail until my next appearance.

My second court date came, and once again, I woke up late. This time, I called and let them know that I woke up late, and was told, in absolute kindness, “No problem. It happens. Thank you for calling and letting us know.”. I made sure that I appeared on time for my third court date. I was given a sentence to serve three days in jail, a stiff fine, and my car impounded. I got the car out before the cost became impossible to afford and had ‘hired’ a lawyer that got me out of serving the three days in jail – which I never did pay all of the money owed for the deed. He saved my ass, and if I knew how to reach him today, I would pay him. I think he’s probably dead now though. He was old when I hired him. He had told me that the judge mistook me to be the son of some woman he had had in court before. All my lawyer had to do was buy lunch to resolve the issue. I felt taken advantage of.

I didn’t give a shit about anything. Even my lateness to appear in court for my DUI didn’t bother me, other than I might end up spending some time in jail. I don’t know what I was living for at the time other than the next day’s drunk.

Schizophrenia - Episode 1

A lot of changes occurred before a major defining moment of my existence took place. I had different roommates that came into being shortly after my first Thanksgiving alone. I had been without a car capable of driving back home to be with my family. I had reached out to a friend after some tears to possibly hang out. His brother had somehow ended up living with him only a few months prior. I found out that he could cook, and we arranged Thanksgiving of our own. He had made a full traditional dinner all the way down to green bean casserole, yams, warm dinner rolls, pumpkin pie... everything you would find on a typical family's table on Thanksgiving. We all became roommates in a townhouse community. Two of my friends in pizza became our next-door neighbors followed by another two shortly after that. We had run a spaghetti network to play video games with each other and had the times of our lives until one fateful day.

I had come home from opening the pizza place. The house was empty and none of my friends were home. I felt eerie being alone in the apartment. I thought I heard kids outside saying that they could see me even though we typically had the shades closed enough that you couldn't peer into the room from outside. I thought that for whatever reason, they were watching me and my every move. I started freaking out, first by pacing the room. I attempted to get closer to the window to hear what they were saying, like I was spying on the spies. I ducked down beneath the window and heard absolutely nothing. I looked out the window. Absolutely nothing. The voices I heard and their source vanished into thin air. I got into my car, and was driving back and forth aimlessly thinking I was hearing people talking, but I couldn't make out what was being said mostly, but I thought that I heard them calling me 'the village idiot' which I would find myself verbally repeating to myself.

I was a mess. I had to have looked frantic to other people. Nobody said anything at first. I wouldn't talk much and barely made eye contact, but I would listen over-intently - trying to examine every word people said. If something didn't sound exactly right, I would twitch and ask them what they said or what they meant. To me, people's conversations seemed like they were trying to play with subliminal messages. Everyone was speaking in code, glancing quickly at me, then continuing to speak. I felt like I was the victim of kind of conspiracy.

I couldn't take it after a while. I was going crazy. I eventually escaped to my room and before I knew it, I was missing days of work. My roommates would try to talk to me, but I drowned them out in thought. Most of their words didn't make it to my ears... just fragments or only a few words.

I don't know how many days blew by. I was smoking so many cigarettes that I thought the overwhelming stench of the smoke smell was actually some kind of toxic gas someone was pumping into my room from a vent behind my bed. I would lay in bed, trying incredibly hard to fall asleep, and too afraid to leave it. I had to leave it though. I had to have my cigarettes. I felt as though I was being followed everywhere I went. It seemed as though there were more cars on the street, more people in the places I went, different people working when I approached the counter to swiftly make my purchase before leaving. I was in the Matrix!

My roommates and friends had somehow found my mom's phone

number and would either call her or have her call, and I would refuse to talk to her. I wasn't going to work and eventually lost my job. After some time, I had gone there demanding to get my job back, was turned down… and gave them hell about it - still not in my right mind. I know that I had to probably look scary. I can't remember exactly how my actions played out, only bits and pieces, but I imagine I came off as a complete madman. I think I said something along the lines of, "So, can I have my job back?" without being prompted to say anything before that… like I was being an asshole. I know I told them to fuck off though when they said "No".

At some point, either my mom or my dad… maybe even both had come to get me and my things. I didn't want to take a single thing, because I thought I was leaving a crime scene or something. Days prior, I rushed into one of my friend's apartments and powered off his computer with him sitting in front of it thinking that people were on the roof trying to use the computers to listen in on us for whatever reason. Later on in this story, this will get even more weird with electronics.

On the way back home (where I grew up), I was filled with fear and not talking even when talked to, I crawled into a little ball in my seat. I felt that I was being swept from danger and had to be hidden to make my escape. My family had to come to extract me from some unknown force out to get me and my job was to stay out of sight.

Not knowing what to do, my mom took me to a mental health institute after a couple of days trying to snap me out of it on her own. The night before she made that decision, I remember trying to get on her computer, logging on to Yahoo Messenger and all the little emojis had strange black eyes and rotten teeth. I immediately went into the living room and curled up into a tight ball on the couch.

I spent about a week in the hospital and for the first time, placed on medications to see what would work to snap me out of my very first schizophrenic episode. My mom and her husband would come, I think my dad came to visit too. I remember being distant and unresponsive. They diagnosed me with schizo-effective disorder, and from that day forth, if questioned by any other doctors, my mom would tell them that that was what I had, what medications seemed to work… and go from there.

I lost contact with my friends for a long time. After some time of being 'better', I had reached out looking for some architecture drawings I had left up there with my other belongings, but having been gone for so long, those things had been tossed in a dumpster.

One of my friends ended up visiting me later with his uncle and I went up once to visit them and that's pretty much it. I found out that my first roommate had had a stroke. I have recently reached out to one saying that I want to visit, but haven't done so yet.

I can only describe this to someone that may have had a similar experience to mine experimenting with marijuana. When I tried it, in a small room with two other guys, it seemed like I could predict exactly what they were going to say before they said it - word for word. I think we got the munchies or something, so we went to a little corner store. While we were in there, I had this overwhelming sense that the clerk and other people might think we're robbing the place. I feared that they thought we'd run up on the clerk and demand everything in the drawer or something and that the cops had been notified and they were on their way.

The major symptoms I feel are sometimes paranoia, usually extreme. I very rarely have visual hallucinations, but I always have audible hallucinations when I have an episode. I hear voices, or sounds will sound like voices - for instance the ticking of a clock might drone a couple words over and over. Sometimes the ticking is ear-piercingly loud, and sometimes I can't hear it at all, no matter how hard I try to listen for it. I feel like I am being watched and that even family members and friends are out to get me. And every time, I don't remember that I have this illness. Every time.

Life in College – Part 2

Once I got into a state of mind that could lead to a productive life, I found myself in an odd moment. I found myself working at a place that I will talk about later, and in a point in my life where I needed guidance. My mom came to speak with me one day. We talked about my interests and what I want to do with my life. I had no clue, and she brainstormed for a minute or two and said, "You always liked computers and you're good at those things, why not go to school for it?". She suggested looking at a community college that was only about a 20-minute walk from where she lived, so, I went and started going after an associate's degree in computer programming and system development.

I worked at night at a 'regular' full-time job, and, during the day, I was a full-time student. I had enough time throughout the day while at school that I could do all the take-home assignments and have very little, if any, left to do after school. I also had a few tiny jobs at the school. I worked in the computer lab as a technician, I became a tutor for a while, and I eventually did work for the school grounds. I did very well and seemingly, it came so naturally, I didn't have to study for tests or anything. I just absorbed everything in the classrooms and did the assigned work.

The girl who disappeared when I lived in Columbus found me on MySpace. We quickly got reunited and obvious things happened. It lasted for a good several months – until one day, I was visiting with her and she had a phone call that ended with her saying, "I love you, too". I immediately left her dorm room but only escaped to the building's computer lab. Not too long after, she followed me there and apologized. I accepted her apology and ended up spending the night, but it wouldn't last much longer. The existence of another man and having to put my feelings on hold anytime he came out of the woodwork would soon destroy whatever fantasy I believed I had at the time.

Shortly into my last semester of that school, one of my professors approached me and was wondering about what I had planned to do after I got my degree and proposed setting up a 2-plus-2 program between the community college and a traditional four-year university. I did so, and later on, pursued my bachelor's degree in computer science, doing equally as well. Only this time, I was now working two full-time jobs while going to school full-time - one job being in my field of study, which I will also discuss shortly.

My drinking, while continuing, seemed to dip during the first few years, but picked right back up once I started working toward my bachelor's degree.

Life in the Workplace – Part 2

Worse than Pizza

I'll say this right now. I don't ever want to hear someone complaining about their job. Not after the one I had to work for almost two years. I can't imagine too many jobs worse than this, although I do know that there are probably quite a few.

My job, for the most part, was to put on a rain suit, and in 34-degree constant temperatures, hose off and scrub large vegetable processing equipment. The chemicals that were used, if combined, I later found out, could kill a person. The fact that the rain suits only lasted a few days before being filled with holes, allowing the person wearing it to become completely soaked for their entire shift, was reason enough to not like the job. The fact that you were thought of as less than a person that deserved a wage at all was the only other belittling thing. In my eyes, we deserved at least double what we got paid.

Everywhere you go, there is at least one person that is full of stories, kinda like me. But, no, we had this one guy that would tell us how successful he was and how he had all this money and nice stuff. He boasted about his car, which was a faded paint, missing hubcaps, four-door Audi. He lived in a trailer. He didn't look or dress like he had much money at all. But we would listen to his stories.

I didn't see too much drug activity, but there were a few people that would sneak off and hit a joint or something and come back. You couldn't tell at all... if you lacked the sense of smell. One night, this one guy on the cleaning crew brought in a little baggie of shrooms. The whole crew, except for me, ate them all and then decided to ditch work and go to the bar down the street and leave me at work all by myself to do all the work. I only cleaned the machines that I typically did, but I had to go around all night pushing broom and shit.

There were a lot of days that we had to work overtime. There were also times that the machines would go days without being cleaned at all because of production requirements. One Christmas Eve, I had to work over and my uncle left me there without a ride. I had to walk home... which was about a 45 minute walk in the cold and snow. Immediately leaving the site, was a 15 minute hike uphill on the road leading toward downtown Wheeling. Eventually, the place got shut down because someone had traced salmonella back to it.

The only good that came out of the entire experience was, that we got a bonus paycheck because the company didn't let us know in advance that we'd all be losing our jobs – something that is required by businesses to do. I also would have had a lifelong friend to play guitar with, but he only got to live a few years after we all lost our jobs. He was a man down on his luck. He lived in low-income housing with a bitch of a girlfriend. He, like myself, had a talent – only his was more as a handyman – and had to decide to find a job regardless of its quality. Later, he decided to try to make a better life for himself by also going back to school. He chose an online university, and upon graduation was doing far better in life than he ever had previously. A path that I was sure that I was also on. He later developed stage four gastrointestinal cancer. They tried chemotherapy and thought that they had put the cancer into remission. A short time later, he died on a beach in the Bahamas.

During most of this time, I lived with either my dad or my mom. When I was staying predominantly at my mom's, I would pay a guy at work to take me to my dad's or take a bus to the bottom of the hill where he lived and walk there – about a 45-minute hike, just so I could play for a few hours on my computer. It was during this time that my grandmother on my biological father's side passed away.

I started to stay at my dad's house more once I paid for the reinstatement fees for my license (four years later) from my DUI.

Second Computer-Related Opportunity

About a month or so before I graduated with my associate's degree, a man from a local business came to the school to discuss a possible job opportunity with people preparing to graduate. I believe that I was the only person dumb enough to show any interest, and within days of graduation, I started to work for this company. The only reason I say that I was dumb with this interest is that the job started out at \$6.00/hr. In one of my classes, it stated in the textbook that an engineer averaged \$35.00/hr and an architect, \$55.00/hr. I would be shorting myself a couple bucks taking this job, but I did it. This could have been a key starting point, but I stayed way too long. I loved the people that I worked with for though, and I was more about security than I am about pay, unfortunately.

My first week almost became my last week at the company. While I knew HTML, CSS, and JavaScript to a certain degree, I was largely unfamiliar with ASP and passing and retrieving information in a web application. That lack of knowledge almost ended my journey prematurely had I not taken a book home from the company and figured those things out. I returned ready to work on the following Monday. The lead programmer was impressed that I figured it out and would tell that story several times over the next 7 or so years.

One of my first tasks was to develop a web browser to scrape data from websites and dump that information into a database that the company's software worked with. My initial browser didn't accomplish that task, but, if any of us had realized it at the time, we would have had tabbed browsing experiences 25 years before it became available to the public - something that I didn't even think would have been revolutionary at the time (actually, I did... even presented it at an Appalachian College Association Convention).

A few months after beginning my time with the company, I was told they couldn't afford to keep me any longer. Before being let go completely, I explained my situation to one of my professors who then pointed me to the Appalachian College Association, which provided me a stipend that allowed me to continue working for the company for a short time, which later led to me being hired on full-time.

It could have been the be-all-end-all project I would have ever had to be a part of, had I known that at the time - kinda... maybe. At the convention, someone asked me what purpose my project could actually achieve. I wonder if he remembers where he first saw that functionality now.

Pizza Person – Part 3

Right around this time, I met and married the woman who would be with me for a long time, but that is something I will discuss later.

During most of my time working on my bachelor's degree, I also found the need to work a second full-time job. That need led me to yet another pizza place where, this time, I used my head a little bit and became a delivery driver instead of taking on any responsibility within the store. I was still a closer though, so I ended up doing most of the cleaning and other tasks when I worked. I still did more than most of the other drivers, including making pizzas and helping count inventory, since I had experience doing so. I was the only driver that did this while the others would simply wait for their deliveries to be ready and end their shift the moment the place wasn't busy anymore.

It was a rat race shit show. The most experienced drivers would steal runs and go out the door with deliveries that they were even expressly told by management they weren't allowed to take. Later, I found out that one driver would purposely leave deliveries in the store for the next guy if he knew that they would result in small, if any, tips. I was usually the guy that ended up with the shit runs. It didn't take too long though. I was competing with this top driver and making good money – until gas went from $2 to $4 per gallon. I would spend more money on gas than I would receive in tips and reimbursement. I left soon after that to work for some old couple claiming to be the number one authors in children's books. I think they bought all of their own books to register any kind of blip on the radar.

The top driver is another death in my history book. He had married a woman who started working at the store. During one of their vacations (honeymoon, I believe), he contracted a flesh-eating amoeba. Not knowing, the doctor prescribed him pain medications for the pains that he had on and around his knee. Later, he passed away. I only happened to have an off-chance meeting with a person at a grocery store that mentioned her last name. I inquired about the guy I knew and was told the news.

Third Computer-Related Opportunity

After completing my degree in computer science, I found an opportunity to work with a sponsored program at the university. I didn't know it existed, and if I had known about it long before I graduated, it might have saved me a lot of money. Working for the university came with the benefit of free tuition for the employees and members of their immediate family.

I brought my wife here to try to get her to finish her degree, but she never did. It's something that would have benefited her greatly, as she hadn't done anything worth doing since shortly after I met her.

When I first started working for this group, I, having most of my experience now in .NET, was told that I couldn't use it. I was allowed to use anything EXCEPT .NET… more or less. Another guy I was in school with that had been working for these guys claimed to know .NET and ruined it for everyone after proving he wasn't so good at it. A quote from this guy that he told one of the content writers was, "The program drives the content.", meaning that the aesthetics of whatever they were making was limited to his lack of knowledge, more or less. The lead programmer told me that the best way to introduce .NET as a skill I possessed was to sneak in some code that worked well on a significant project.

Largely, everything that I worked on dealt with data-driven websites. Some of the projects were clever sites designed to take input from students and pass that information to individuals belonging to the sponsored programs I worked for – seemingly in real time.

The lead programmer concocted some of these projects using simple PHP scripts using MySQL to store and retrieve information that got passed back and forth based on timers. I took that to the next level by building a Web Service, something I was familiar with coming from my last place of employment and injecting the service into a FlashBuilder project that I was going to be working on. I used it one or two more times and then shelved it. The projects that I put into use never left the office, but would have been very successful had they used them, I believe.

After showing that I did, indeed, possess enough skills in .NET, I was never questioned again. Prior to this, I was tasked with building a website used to gather data from individuals on NASA-related projects. I was told to build this using a personal desktop product called FileMaker Pro. While it had the capability of storing information and later, displaying it to someone else, it didn't have the functionality of a true website capable of handling a multitude of users accessing it simultaneously. In fact, only 5 simultaneous users could attach to it at any given time. Regardless, I finished the project. It was then to be sold to some other company that was taking over the project, and they rejected the FileMaker Pro approach... something I warned about, complained about, and shed tears over... the entire time I worked on it. It looked pretty though. An employee that they had at the time (someone I had a major crush on and probably still do) could literally make dog shit look like a dessert – and provided me with the graphics and color scheme that it needed to have.

About three years after starting to work for these guys, my wife and I had a daughter. It was a joy that I was allowed to enter my workplace. She would stop by with her wrapped in a blanket and everyone cooed over her. It was a happy time at work. But that birth and beauty in our life seemed to have an adverse effect on the marriage – which seemed to spiral down into oblivion ever since until it ultimately ended in divorce – something I'll cover later.

In 2013, President Obama established a sequestration that stopped government funding from being used to fund programs such as ours, and one of the sponsored programs I worked with dissolved almost entirely, saving a small handful of people still working on the money from existing grants.

I immediately shifted gears and worked on the other sponsored program projects and stayed in the same cubicle for a few more years.

My time with these sponsored programs was full of love and life. Everyone seemed to care for everyone else. It really was one of those job opportunities where everyone treated everyone else like family.

After my time with these guys, I would come back in the future to try to write a new version of one of their most popular products at no cost, in hopes that it would bring my coding abilities current to the times. I accomplished that, but I failed to provide them, ultimately, with a working product. It worked locally on my gear, but for some reason, we couldn't get it to work on the servers. I didn't know anything about hosting software, so, I could only research and propose solutions that never panned out. If I were allowed to work on it again, I could provide them with one of the best software products that they could possibly possess. (Embellishing? Maybe.)

Schizophrenia - Episode 2

As my days in the sponsored programs were diving into a regrettable end, I was job seeking and had an interview with a company that looked promising, but before finding out whether I would get that job, I had another schizophrenic episode that led to me being hospitalized again. I believe that this would be the first time that the regulations of this type of hospitalization had changed where a patient was not released until a thorough check on their well-being had been performed and after a considerable amount of observation took place – often leading to a much longer stay than when I first started having episodes requiring hospitalization.

This episode was in the months of probably November and up until almost the end of December. I received word from the company I had been chosen for the position. I immediately began to act like I was doing much better and begging that I be released because if I didn't accept the position soon, I would lose the opportunity. I was released and went to work in Columbus. I had to stay with these two guys that had an apartment. I lasted two weeks at the company and relapsed hardcore. I can't remember if I got placed back into care upon returning home or not. I was doing ok for the first few days.

The work was not difficult, and I was doing well, but all of a sudden, I felt as though people were talking about me among st themselves - and not in a good way. I couldn't hear what was said entirely, but it seemed like I would pick out some words and assumed it all had to do with me.

I do remember all of my family members coming to visit me in the hospital prior to leaving the hospital for this job. My daughter was only about five at the time. So much love was conveyed, and all I could do was sit there in fear. It would go away though, before being let out, and I would start making phone calls to them when they couldn't visit and chitchat on the phone as long as they'd allow me.

In all of my hospital stays, crafts usually bring me out of my state of mind the easiest – on top of the medications. I don't know why, but maybe creativity is an escape from reality more than some people give it credit, but, in the medical realm, it is widely known.

There was at least one prior short stay in a hospital years before this took place. I don't remember anything about my state of mind, but I remember being in the suicide watch wing the first day that I was in there. I remember that we were allowed to go outside to smoke back then, but later, they removed that privilege.

Shortly after this, I had my second DUI. I was on my way back from the store to buy more beer and passed a car with someone driving well under the speed limit on a solid yellow line street. You're not allowed to pass, and unbeknownst to me, the person in my rear-view was a police officer. If I hadn't learned my lesson a long time ago, this would have been a second chance. Seems that most of my second chances are wrought with the same wrong decisions as the first.

As a Lover – Part 2

My wife found me online. I believe it was on MySpace, but she reached out to me first, believing (or so she said), that I was an instructor at one of the colleges that she found on my profile. We began talking. I told her that her profile picture made her look as if she was perpetually bored. We exchanged some text and talked on the phone a few times and then met about a week or so later. She probably wanted to tidy up around the house a bit. Knowing what I know now, that was most likely the reason for the delay.

She rented a small 2-story home with a basement in a town nearby. She lived in spitting distance of her parents. She also painted a portion of the interior baby blue, much to the dismay of the landlord. Upon seeing the room adjacent to her bedroom, I quickly realized what the week-long wait entailed, but thought very little about it.

I was going to school and working two full-time jobs and when I'd appear at the end of a long day at her home, which I was living in, after a few months of seeing her, I would go to the computer to do some work and she'd immediately find a reason to use the computer so that I couldn't. It wasn't my computer, so I didn't have much I could say, but it should have been a tell-tale sign of the relationship I was getting into.

We did a lot of things together. We'd go out to movies and dinners. We went to nightclubs, mostly to see a person she knew playing with his band live. He was a singer, and every night, he'd make some unlucky girl in the crowd uneasy when he would announce his undying love for her. At the time, it was my wife's sister, but after repeatedly being rejected, that longing for her faded and some other unlikely person became the love interest of a man simply trying to tie the knot with anyone that would accept him… she had to be amazingly beautiful though. He'd often come to me for relationship advice. At that time, and pretty much from then on, I should have been the last person anyone would want to receive advice about love from.

Life was fun, and for what it is worth, it seemed that I had found that missing piece of a puzzle known as life. A few years later, we would have a child of our own, and everything seemed to fall into place, for a short while. I was getting my education and thought that my life could only go up from where it had crawled out of a hole only a few years prior. But that would indefinitely prove to be the wrong way to view that moment in time.

My mom, who had become an ordained priest, was the person I chose to have marry us. I thought it was the greatest thing in the world – something that not many people can probably say about their marriages. Shortly after marrying us, maybe a few years… my mom and her husband moved to Montana – where he later died from cirrhosis of the liver caused in part by taking a particular blood pressure medication.

My grandmother on her side passed away before she moved to Montana, and she performed the service. So, she has married and buried her own family - something she never thought she would have the willingness to do. All I can say is tears… a lot of tears.

Our daughter had colic and cried a lot. My wife would stay most of the time in the room in a rocking chair and try to get her to sleep. I'd be a drunken mess and go pass out in the bed in what would have been our room still. She ended up becoming that mother who sleeps with their child forever. They probably still sleep in the same bed. I don't know. I don't ask.

Seemingly to me, that is when our relationship started to go downhill. Our daughter filled my wife's life, and a bottle of beer in hand and playing a video game filled mine. We used to play video games together, but after childbirth, only I kept those pixels dancing. I should have taken the cue and became more of a husband and father at that point, but alcohol had me in its grasp and playing video games was largely a part of my life for a long time, and still is. I regret much of my life during this time now, and as time went on, things only got worse. My work life was always unstable. My drinking only grew worse. My love for my wife waned. And my love for my daughter, although ever-present, didn't lend me to be at her side nearly as much as it should have. I've cried over this countless times, both in her presence as well as in solitude. Today, the realization that I lost so much time of a very important part of both of our lives lies heavy on my heart and soul. In an attempt to revitalize that lost childhood, I am finding myself talking to a person who is quickly approaching adulthood, and realizing it is probably too late to rekindle that childhood feeling for her. I am either grateful that she doesn't hate me for that past, or she hides it too well and I am ignorant of the fact.

As an alcoholic, I was mouthy. She had her flaws, but I also had mine. We probably fought more than we loved, or so it seemed. We treated each other more like roommates and less like people who loved each other. In my head, I thought I was doing everything right though. And only after being ripped away from a never-ending bottle of beer, do I realize what I've done so wrong.

Before having our daughter, I had moved us into a home with a mortgage rather than renting from someone else. I figured that if we were going to fork out money, might as well be for something that we could eventually own. Rent is ridiculous anyway, the way the cost goes up seemingly every other month.

Schizophrenia – Episode 3

My wife was told about my condition. My mom tried to instruct her how to tell if an episode was coming on and what signs to look for. She has spotted it coming on a few times before. She's been able to snap me out of it once or twice, but I finally ended up in the hospital again - another month-long stint in a familiar place. I relapsed after showing good signs of recovery which prompted another week on the inside. I had a habit of dropping off of my medications. Everyone could see the pattern but me. It was the first time I believed I had done something to make my wife cry. It was a confession I had made about doing something that I won't go into here, but it was an act of betrayal that she shouldn't have had to endure. The fact that our relationship remained intact afterward was amazing, but it never made things much better.

I don't know why staying on medication was so difficult. Actually, the stability of my career had a large part to do with it. I'd be on and off of work so often, that I found periods of unemployment where I didn't have the insurance or the cash to pay for them. It was a vicious cycle in that regard, but I also had this feeling that if I was feeling ok, then I must not have to take medicines. It was some sort of false thinking - instead of thinking that I am doing ok because I am on medication, I was believing that I was ok and didn't need them.

I had been in the hospital a few more times before this episode. The reason I don't have a chapter for every episode is that some of them I can't remember too many details, or the episode was minor, or short-lived. I'll have many to talk about near the end of the book that I can go into a little more detail about.

The hardest part about this episode was that it resulted in sorrow for someone outside of myself. I had made my wife cry over something I had done and when I saw the tears flowing down her cheeks, I wanted to console her, but at the same time, I didn't feel as though I had a right to. All I could do is sit there in shame as she talked to the nurse at the station.

As a Parent – Part 1

I had believed that I was a good father. I loved my daughter to death, but at the same time, much of my focus was on beer and video games. She would come downstairs and play around on the computer doing things like swimming or flying with my characters but would soon be called back upstairs by her mom. I would get angry but never said anything. I didn't see anything wrong with her coming downstairs to hang out with me.

Being upstairs on the couch with my wife did nothing but stir arguments. I would have to listen to complaints about the beer or how much I smelled like smoke. I'd have to listen to them both asking me if I had to make 'those noises'... I have had a sinus problem ever since I was a small child. I didn't care for how messy the house got over time... it irritated me that in order to sit on the couch with my family, shit had to be thrown on the floor to make room. All of it just made it harder to be a member of the family, and out of everyone, my daughter got the short end of the stick.

My daughter and I would play board games every so often, and for a while, she would read me chapters out of her children's bible.. I was a proud daddy when she was able to set up a chess board and play. She didn't play outside at home very often, but there were some fun moments. One year, she created a fairy garden in the yard by the porch. I wish she would have kept doing that every year, but she didn't. I miss those days

She wrote stories and still does to this day. She has been writing since about the age of five and that is her lifelong dream – to be an author/illustrator. I have lost track of all of her stories. I used to ask to read them either as she progressed through them or after they were finished. I know that she's got a ton that I didn't know she even wrote. She's creative and I believe that if I can write this story, then she can be successful doing her thing for a living. I have that confidence that you find in most parents because I've seen her in action.

I don't know how we got lucky with her. Growing up, it seemed that I was often at the receiving end of discipline, but I have never had to do ANYTHING to discipline my daughter. I've never seen her get yelled at by anyone else or get her butt spanked like I got when I was growing up. She was just born with an innate ability to always be on her best behavior. I only know of one instance where she did get disciplined, but I wasn't there when it happened. Supposedly she acted up in a store and her mom took her to the bathroom and whacked her butt. I never seen any bad behavior. She is very polite and always caring. She's a miracle child!

Since my divorce, I have learned that she was getting bullied at the public school she was attending. As a remedy, my ex-wife has enrolled her in a private Christian school. She has fewer people in her class, I think it's like six people. She says she gets along with all of them, which is very good to hear. The only thing is, taking her out of her old school wouldn't have been my approach. I believe it encourages her to run away from her problems rather than confront them.

I am somewhat displeased that she was largely deprived of what I would consider a childhood. She never really got to go outside and play with friends. She wasn't allowed to go on field trips with the class - which after a while, she would shrug off as if she didn't want to go in the first place. Just one thing after another, that defined childhood in my head, was stripped away from her and all she was left with was a protective bubble so thick that she couldn't see the outside world from within it.

Her playtime was reduced to seclusion or hanging out with her cousin. They don't get along great all the time... but just well enough that she isn't completely bored and devoid of social interaction. I don't get it. I was almost forced to go outside and play when I was little. Things have changed since my childhood, and I think for the worse. It gives her all the opportunity she needs to live in her world and write stories though. I guess a lot of loss in interaction lends itself greatly to creativity.

I found out that when she was younger, she had an imaginary dad who played with her all the time. Hearing about that hit me like a ton of bricks. It's one of those things that I had to hear though.

Holidays were always great - especially Christmas. I didn't go out shopping for her gifts, her mom did most of that. She'd buy things all throughout the year and hide them all over the house - sometimes to remain hidden for years. It was funny, and I am shocked that our daughter didn't uncover some of them.

We played hide-and-seek a lot in the house. The house is like... 800 sq ft - two bedrooms, one real bathroom, a kitchen, living room, basement, and an attached garage. It didn't provide very many possibilities for hiding spots, but I always had one that I could utilize that for some reason, she never learned to look for me there. It was great, and my wife would get involved almost all the times we played it. One time, our daughter fell asleep in her awesome hiding spot. I looked everywhere and couldn't find her. Finally, my wife lifted up some blankets or clothes and she was laying in there fast asleep. It was the cutest thing!

If I could offer anyone any amount of advice: don't take these years for granted. Don't do like I did and sit there and think you have plenty of time. You don't, and you never get those moments back, no matter how much you want to.

Life in the Workplace – Part 3

Within this time, I had a few more losses in my world. One of my uncles passed away in his home. He was a military man – Air Force. He was into technology and I believe that he was going into the private sector, and shortly after passed away. He was known not to take good care of himself and didn't take it upon himself to get checked out regularly. It was one of those moments that nobody saw coming, however.

The second loss was my friend from that shit hole job that I already discussed.

My mom's husband, whom I have talked about briefly.

And finally, my aunt. She had a procedure done – a simple colonoscopy – that some of us believe led to an infection that went septic. I was working for the coal company that I will talk about soon when she was sent to the hospital. By the time I got there, she only had a few more minutes of life left. It was one of the most gut-wrenching moments of my life. All any of us could do was stand there and watch as the last bit of life in her left her body in violent convulsions. Her funeral would be the first that my daughter would have to see. She didn't know much about death if anything. I can only think that it was more traumatic for her than she let people see.

My teeth started to get really bad right before I had left Columbus. By the time I get to the retail job in this section, my teeth were mostly black and chipping and in very bad shape. While I was at the retail job, my aunt and uncle began helping me to have them taken out to get dentures. The top plate is very good, but the bottom plate is basically useless. I can't use the bottom plate to chew. They move around too much, causing sores and a lot of pain.

The Many Short-Term Failures

I had so many very short experiences in various jobs. I had so many failed interviews that I should have learned enough to know how to ace them all. I didn't get anything from the experiences that I did have. I didn't learn anything from the work I was doing, and I never went beyond what I learned in college to learn anything new up to this point.

One interview I went to, I had a temporary bottom denture. I had to converse with five different groups in the workplace before finally talking with the head of the department. This denture was floating around in my face so bad that I had to apologize to these people. I was so fucking embarrassed and I bet that they laughed and talked about me after I left. I am surprised that they didn't laugh to my face.

I thought I was going to do well with a mortgage company. I had been brought in and started out to fulfill support tickets. Most of the work was automated with little scripts, so there was no learning involved. I quickly started to get requests to create ad-hoc SQL queries to generate reports. I competed with another guy doing the same stuff as me. We were both brought on as contractors and fighting over the same handful of tickets every day. Once I began cranking out a few, he'd hurry up and gobble them all up, probably not even completing them before closing them out, so he'd be the better employee choice if either of us were to get hired on full time. I also began to get coding assignments. I don't think I did anything significant, and if I had more than one task that never made it past quality control, I can't remember. Like a lot of jobs, before and after this one, I was brought into an office and told I was being let go because the company couldn't afford to keep me around.

After multiple bad experiences, I returned to that cozy center of my galaxy at the university I graduated from to pitch an idea to bring all of their 'missions' up to date. They called their software and scripts missions. The software was nothing more than real-time data websites. I've been familiar with them and have written some of them. My idea was to redo them using 'today's' coding platforms and standards and bring about more appealing experiences for both the team of the sponsored program and the students engaged with them.

The pitch was sweet. I would create one, end to end, and then after successfully deploying that project, I would then go about building the rest of the missions for a little bit of money each. I thought the prices that I offered to do them were inadequate for the job, but it seemed to be the only steppingstone I had to get out of a hole.

That first project was nearly complete, when, for some stupid reason, I decided to update all of the 3rd party packages in my bundle – thereby crippling the software to the point that it would no longer run on the server that I was intending to deploy it to. Nothing that I nor the IT guy running the server did to remedy the situation worked. Shortly afterward, I had another schizophrenic experience that halted my going to their aid and getting my software to work. When I finally got out of my bad state, they no longer wished to partner up with me to get things back on track.

Short-Term Salvation – Part 1

Before working on software for the sponsored program, I found myself applying for and being accepted by a company in the coal industry. This company has brought about a friendship that exists still today. The job was trash. It was comprised of a bunch of people that planned to grow old and retire barely ever accomplishing anything.

The company had a software need for a basic business application. The group would build out a few features in one package and then adopt a new entirely different architecture and language to do it all over again.

When I first started, I began working on frivolous things like 'automated testing'. The project was bullshit. I wrote some VB code that would execute some stored procedures and see if they passed or failed. I didn't remember much from the old days when I played with threading a VB application, so, instead of a bunch of processes running all at once, the entire thing ran sequentially, which took an absurd amount of time.

My next task wasn't too bad though. I was working inside the software building a scheduling system. It consisted of a calendar where shipments could be scheduled and tracked. It was thick though – kind of clunky. I wouldn't want to use it if it was part of my daily routine. The other guys in the group guided me to it, and it was something they approved of, but eventually, it got dumped along with the rest of the software of that iteration shortly after I was let go – because... you guessed it: insufficient funds. For what it's worth, it was only supposed to be a six-month contract, but it got stretched out a few additional months before it ended.

I remember ratting out some punk kid employee that would just work on whatever he wanted and did things however he wanted to do them, even when told specifically how it was supposed to be done. He had gotten his ass handed to him in a conversation about it and when he left the room, a few of us were close enough to hear him talking shit. He didn't last too much longer in the company. I think he asked my buddy about it. If I remember correctly, he didn't like me after that.

The Retail Experience

Like some of my other experiences, my last job didn't equate to me having available unemployment benefits. I had to find a job, and fast. I was married and I had put my family into a real house with a mortgage payment rather than having a rental agreement. With no time to lose, I began going door to door filling out job applications. I tried pizza places, gas stations, and grocery stores while I was also applying to software development jobs on Indeed and LinkedIn. No longer did a company with an unskilled laborer position open want a person with my level of experience and education. To them, I was a ticking time bomb. One phone call, and I would be off somewhere else making a lot more money.

Then along came a wonderful retail position. I applied for a position working in their photo lab and got hired on. ASAP wasn't nearly as fast as I needed it to be, but it came. It seemed like we were just barely keeping our heads above water... and a lot of time was spent with our heads beneath it.

In having this position, I realized that my eyesight was a lot worse than I imagined. I would have to look at tiny, faded text and try to piece orders together or read SKUs when helping other departments put out new goods or rearrange shelves. It was bad enough that I got an eye exam and had a prescription lens made. I was now wearing bifocals for the first time in my life. But even with them on, they did very little to improve the very task which prompted me to get them in the first place. I soon stopped wearing them altogether, and today, I would say my eyesight is better than it was back then... but I could be lying to all of us. I don't know.

When I first started working there, the person that was in charge was an older lady. It was typically just her and I in the lab working. I don't recall having other employees around, and we handled it pretty well. Also, it was kinda like helping your grandma in the kitchen, as she didn't care if you made mistakes here and there.

I have a lot of interesting stories about this place. Perhaps, even without mentioning the name of the place, you will know which company it is - based solely on the stereotyped customers I will mention.

Being in the photo lab meant a lot of things. You're somehow the goto person for telling customers where every item in the store is located. You get all the calls to the store from people wanting to know about everything other than photo products and services. And you're in a good spot to see just about anything you can think of - people in pajamas, clothing that either reveals too much skin or is so tight the bodies wearing them could be used as dolls in front of an anatomy class, and nude photos that they want to have printed out... which is against our policy - and they will bitch and complain about it.

Being in a retail store, I always wondered if they sent secret agents or mystery shoppers around the store. One day, I was walking back to the photo lab and there were two beautiful blonde women, both wearing white tank tops and blue jean shorts. I don't know how loud I said it, but I think they might have heard me say, "Damn!" all drawn out and shit. They immediately came over to me and wanted to print out a photo and pick out a frame in the aisles directly in front of the lab. While they were getting their phones ready, they let me know that they'd need help getting everything set up, and while I was plugging in their phone and following all the prompts, they both start kinda standing too close and brushing up against me. I was already turned on by them before that, and I really had to control myself. After they picked out their picture and sent the print job, they both walked off a couple feet away and were talking to each other in Russian or some other similar language. It's odd that that didn't trigger some kind of schizophrenic episode. They looked pretty young... if they were of legal age, they weren't too much older than 18.

People will print anything. I never followed the rules strictly for leafing through every photo. After the older woman left the lab, they hired a new manager of the department: a younger woman that ran that ship tight! One of her top problems with me was that I didn't look at the photos. She actually threatened my job over it. I would pretend to do the task when she was around, but would skip the task when she was out of sight. I didn't feel right invading other people's privacy. I did know that there were reasons to check the photos though. There could be bad prints, there could be indecent photos, there could be illegal photos, and so on. She would catch me too. She'd purposely wander off during a print job and come back just as it was finishing to catch me stuffing envelopes without looking at them and scold me.

One day, a chic came in and was printing off a small bundle of photos: maybe ten pictures tops. I didn't grab that batch, the manager did and was looking through them. One of the photos was a nude photo. She pointed it out to me and told me that that was why we need to be checking them. She shredded the photo, but I had to be the person that handed the prints to the customer and explain why we shredded the photo. This girl would come in several times again throughout the next few weeks trying to squeak out naughty pics. Sometimes I would catch them, sometimes she'd show up to pick some up that I didn't look through. After a while, I would recognize her name and know to look for them. She stopped coming shortly after that.

Two incidents occurred where a customer would come up to the lab and need help printing photos from the kiosks.

The first time, it was a guy. He pulled up his photos and there are countless photos of him with a woman, both naked. He didn't even flinch... he just pointed them out and was like, "Kitchen. Dining Room, Washing Machine..." naming off where he was doing this chic. It was funny as hell, but I had to tell him he couldn't print those. He said that those weren't the photos he was going to print out. He was just bragging, because the girl in the photo was pretty hot.

The second time, it was a woman. She had much nicer pics than the guy I just talked about. Over a thousand pictures, a screen filled with nothing but close-up nudes of every inch of her being. She quickly unplugged her phone, but it was too late. I had seen everything. She told me that she was so embarrassed and then quickly walked away. I figured that I probably would be embarrassed too. She must not have been too embarrassed though, because about ten minutes later, she came back - after hiding the good pics. She acted as though nothing at all happened just moments before. I helped her get set up again and she was off to the races.

This job is historic in the world of Ruckman. I have met gays and lesbians, but I had never seen a transgender in person before, and I haven't since. It was during Black Friday. People are everywhere tackling each other for the best deals and then… there's this 8 foot tall wookie wearing a yellow sun dress complete with a hat and heavy makeup just standing there seemingly gazing off into the distance hoping to appreciate the landscape of Paris or some shit. Nobody said anything, no laughter, nothing. It was like nobody even noticed. So, knowing what I have seen since Trump took office, maybe if these people would have just gone about their business, there wouldn't be any problems. I do like that some of them will argue that you can't tell if a person is trans or not. Well, all I know is he looked like a turkey with that Adam's Apple sticking out plain as day.

Another problem that my manager had with me is how well I cleaned the printers at the end of the night. I couldn't get those things to pass her white glove test no matter what I did. I am not sure if that was even necessary, but she did it like once a week to me. Literally, the process is to take a little hand vacuum to the surfaces of the printer. That isn't going to clean it completely.

I think I was with this place for a little over a year before I reached out back to the coal people. I arranged a get-together with the crew that I worked with and took another job with them - this time,. as a full-time employee.

Short-Term Salvation – Part 2

Back in the saddle, I found out what I had only been told about before. They truly recycle and reiterate entire stages of development. Where they were working with VB.NET and Web Forms before, they were now using C# and MVC. They also implemented Web Services. I don't know if they had them before or not, but they had them now. They used a 3rd party front-end package called Telerik also… I made fun of that junk the whole time I was there. I was always one that believed in creating things from scratch.

First, I was working on a piece of software that they wanted nested controls. So, almost like a paged data grid with child nodes that drilled down into more specific details. It was hideous. It worked, but it was slow. Everything about the software was slow, and I didn't know why. They also tacked on search criteria. There were so many parameters that after I had finished that project, they broke my pages into multiple separate project links with less search criteria to make it easier for the end-users to understand.

After that, I was tasked with a few other similar projects within the software, and then they finally ended up with a 'brilliant' idea, not… to work on Visualization. The lead programmer wanted graphs and charts and data! OK. what data? They didn't know. I had to something and show it to them and they'd tell me if they wanted to keep it. That went on for quite some time, but it never became more than an afterthought from the people we presented it to. Everything about it was appealing, but bottom-of-the-bucket not important.

These people have been waiting FOREVER for a minimum viable

product, and we show them charts and graphs representing a very small portion of an incomplete product that didn't achieve anything in the two years I have been there. I'd be pissed. However, I never saw bad feelings being conveyed to anyone. If they proved to be productive, they were safe.

I don't remember when I started doing it, but I didn't find it necessary to show up to punch in early. I would keep the car running with the heat on in the parking lot and sit there with my eyes closed until it was almost 8:00 AM and then walk in, punch in, put my stuff on my desk and then go to the restroom if I needed to, put on a pot of coffee if it wasn't already being made, and return to my desk with a cup of coffee. This went on for months, but I finally got my ass chewed for it. The Kitty Calendar person supposedly in charge of our department came barging in yelling at me for not showing up early, prepared for work. He had a spreadsheet with my time punches and video evidence of when I punched in and punched out - so he said. He even claimed that one time, I showed up fifteen minutes late. He berated me, saying that if I don't think the job is important enough to show up on time, that I can look for another job. For the next few days or so, I think I showed up fifteen minutes early every day, sat at my desk for anywhere between fifteen minutes and an hour and a half and then would go to his office and tell him I was going home because I didn't feel well. It didn't take long that I was brought into an office, just like any other instance in my career, and let go – because not only did they not have money – they were going into bankruptcy. Kitty Calendar and the entire development team were standing in the room when I came back to gather my things. They said that they had nothing to do with it, proving to me that they did.

The lead programmer's son, who happened to do a 1-month internship with us – who couldn't put functional text boxes on a screen – got hired on full-time in my stead three months after I was let go. I wrote a nasty email to them. I said that except for one of them, they couldn't program their way out of a wet paper bag. I stand by that still today. The project that they need to build should have taken no more than one year to complete. I was there two times, and they never got to more than 25% completion.

End of the Line

So, there I was. I was lucky enough to have worked during a period which allowed me to be on Unemployment, and this was at the onset of COVID, so on top of my benefits, I was also receiving a stimulus check. In total, I was receiving more money than at any time in my employment history. However, this was short-lived. I had to find something within six months, and I wasn't having much luck.

After unemployment ran out and the stimies stopped coming, I was forced with one of the harshest realities any man could face, aside from death itself. We were months behind on almost every bill that we had and were receiving help from her parents (from what she told me) at one point, and my aunt and uncle after her parents stopped helping us. Our marriage was rocky at best but still enduring. We finally hit rock bottom. She was taking our daughter to her parents' house to eat and get cleaned up. I was making weekly trips to the food pantry to stand in line with homeless people for a bit of bread growing moldy and a few cans of vegetables that would end up being my meals for the week. It wasn't enough for just me, let alone all of us.

Alcohol – The Downward Spiral – Part 2

By this time in my life, I had elevated my drinking from one 12-pack of beer per day to almost a case. Where I once used to find myself to my bed before passing out, I wasn't making it out of the basement. When I was too poor to buy a lot of beer, I would buy the most powerful beer on the market. More than five would have me passed out in the yard, and I found myself resorting to that more often than not.

A long time ago, before the doctors discovered that my biological father was full-blown schizophrenic, they believed that perhaps my drinking of alcohol created a chemical imbalance in my brain that caused my episodes. If that were true, only during this time in my life would I attribute my level of drinking to some illness other than simply alcoholism.

During this time, I would bring my daughter outside and cry to her, apologizing for my failures as a father. I never felt as rock-bottom as I did during this stage. Had it not been for a family intervention that was coming to me soon, I don't know what would have happened to me.

Life in the Workplace – Part 4

What could have become a miracle, will later in this story, prove to be nothing but brutal misery.

As I began a path of despair, a notification lit up on LinkedIn, or maybe it was an email, from a company claiming that they wanted to interview me for an Android position that they had. I expressed that I did not have experience with mobile development, but they insisted that I would be put through training. I didn't have to think long and hard on the subject.

Unfortunately, you will have to wait to find out the details of this for a future book release. I am currently involved in a lawsuit with the company in question.

Schizophrenia – Episode 4

During my second contract at the company that is currently taking me to court, I woke up one morning thinking I was hearing very loud death metal music. Shortly after that, I believed I was being scolded by first, my wife's mother, and then by my own. I screamed at the voices in retaliation. My wife woke up and asked me who I was screaming at and I replied, "My mom, your mom, you…". Out of fear, she grabbed our daughter and they left the house, probably to go to my mother-in-law's house. That would be the last time I spent the night in my own home.

Shortly after they left the house, I left too. I didn't know where I was going, but I went barefoot, leaving my coat, shoes, phone, and keys all either in the house, or strewn along the gravel road that led to our house. On my way to nowhere in particular, I passed the school that my daughter went to, sat down by a pillar displaying their mascot, and cried for what I believe was a half hour. All the while, I was hearing voices, which started out harsh, but ended up consoling and then encouraging. The voices had me believe that the best things in my life were about to take place. I got up and in a fit of justification, anxiously awaited someone to pull up to me and offer me a Ferrari and a load of money or something.

People driving by didn't seem to want to stop for me, however. One person coming up alongside me from a side street stopped at the stop sign and I jumped into the vehicle and told them to take me where they were going to take me. She jumped out of the vehicle and the next thing I knew, cops were there. I was asking them to take me somewhere secure where we could talk because out in the open, Google could hear what we discussed and I would be in trouble. They told me not to move, but I didn't listen. I was somewhere between panic and compliance, or they would have probably cuffed me.

They took me to a hospital. I don't know which one. I was hearing voices, but as much as I tried at first to understand what they were saying, I couldn't. There was a lot of beeping and buzzing sounds, and in my head, they signified dread. I thought I had to do silly things, like hold my breath and not make a single movement or sound when I heard them. Everything would have been fine if I weren't visibly shaking.

I don't think they did anything with me with medication. They did bring me a meal and some juice. I was afraid to touch it. I felt like it was a trap if I ate any of the food. I reached for the juice and took a small drink. Finding out that nothing bad happened, I grabbed a sandwich and started eating.

After a few hours, I asked that my wife be called and to have her bring me my jacket and shoes. She never showed up. My uncle arrived and we went to his house, which later I would discover would be my new home.

I don't remember what happened after I got into my uncle's car. I remember getting to his house, but everything else in between is gone. I don't remember. I don't recall leaving the house once I got there, but I did.

I discovered that my wife had a restraining order on me after arriving on the gravel road leading to the house. I don't know how the cops knew I was there, but they pulled up behind me and filled me in. I don't remember how I got there or how I left, or where I even came from when I arrived. This is the hard part, because unlike the majority of the rest of my life, things are blank to me now. I only recall small bits and pieces here and there.

I still tried to work on the contract in my altered state. It didn't take long before I ended up in the hospital again, where everyone thought I had abandoned my contracts. Once they were back in contact with me, they threatened me with a lawsuit if I didn't immediately sign another 2-year contract with them and begin the interview process all over again.

At one point, after moving in with my uncle, I left the house. It was nighttime, and I don't know where my uncle was. I think he could have been visiting one of his neighbor friends. I was going in and out of the house smoking a lot. Seemingly, the tv was playing a trick on me. I would catch the characters talking as if they were watching me and trying to confuse me. I'd catch them saying one thing that sounded twisted, rush outside, come back in a few minutes later and catch them sounding normal for a split second then returning to twisted again. I took my cell phone and sitting on the floor facing away from the TV, I made several recordings to prove that I wasn't crazy. Crazy, huh? I had proof that something incredibly wrong was going on.

I don't recall what time it was. I ended up in the town that my wife lived in, parked my car in front of a police vehicle - blocking it in the parking lot. I tossed the keys of my car on to the building to my left, and my cell phone on the police building. I was there probably at least an hour, perhaps longer. I was delirious and was believing that my wife and daughter and all of their belongings were now being transported, in full, so that I would never be able to see them again. The people on the TV were planning it, and I had proof of it on my phone. A police officer arrived and I am very surprised that I didn't end up sitting in a jail cell. That situation, I believe, could have escalated out of control in a very short amount of time. I was not acting rational at all. At one point, I felt that I had to hit the officer in order for him to believe me, or arrest me. I wasn't going to, but my actions could have probably been thought of as aggressive. At one point, I turned away from the officer and then turned back around, and it looked like he was giving me the finger. He told me to move my car. I told him that I threw them. He had me look along the building in case they landed on the ground and not on the roof.

I believe he called someone on the CB. After not being able to find my keys, and it was, at that point, obvious I was in an altered mental state, he offered to have me taken to a hospital. Another trip to the hospital, which I believe that I walked out of shortly after arriving. I believe that during this time, I ended up in the streets near a corner store and might have gotten into a fight with some innocent dude returning to his car. I do not know if this was a real occurrence or dreamed up, but I don't remember anything after that involving the incident.

I would end up back in another hospital soon though. I was having this sensation that the main room with the TV and the tables where we ate were somehow divided into sections. One section was for truth and justice and one section would be for evil things. It's hard to explain. But if I wanted to be a 'good boy', I would sit at one of the tables and if I wanted to seek revenge or something, I'd have to sit on the couch and watch TV, which at the time, I believe was showing a crime show. Later, there was a Marvel movie something with Ten Rings. When that came on, I felt like I needed to go sit over there and watch the movie. The dialogue didn't match the video to me. The words, I wish I could play them side-by-side, would not be the words of the movie, but something different… and unintelligible. This happens a lot to me - especially around a digital device capable of producing sound. My uncle's police scanner, the TV, a computer… almost any consumer electronics device can be extremely scary to me.

During my time in the hospital this time around, I had missed a court appearance to discuss the restraining order. Missing that appearance elevated my restraining order to an order of protection. I didn't know anything about a court appearance, but ever since this recent event, for the next several months (from November of 2021 to June 2022), I would hear voices saying that I had to go to court. Everyone I had ever known, even those I have only ever said 'hi' to would end up in prison, and I would have to wander the earth visiting every courthouse and stand trial after trial. I wouldn't have a scheduled court case. I would have to burst into the courtroom and prove that I needed to be on trial. Several voices popped in my head. I was talking about Guantanamo Bay, something about Martial Law, and I kept hearing a voice over and over saying, "You're going to pay for what you did to this company!", especially when I would go outside to smoke. Early on in this book, I mention that I had thoughts that I could foresee the future. This is what I was talking about.

Shortly after all of this, I received papers for the dissolution of my marriage. I couldn't comprehend it. I didn't ask for help deciphering it. I merely signed it, not knowing what the consequences would be. It wouldn't be the last time that I signed something that would thoroughly fuck me over, either. I had to appear in court for the dissolution. So, there was one court case that came about, almost like it was prophesied.

I had been in and out of hospitals for a solid eight months, the final time lasting over two months. I had been attempting repeatedly to run off from my uncle's home claiming that I had to appear in court. At moments when I was alone in the home, I would go room to room trying to find something that might end my life fast enough to be beyond salvageable should anyone find me. I figured that if I was dead, then, of course, I wouldn't have to wander the earth going to court and my family and friends wouldn't have to go to prison.

None of this, especially my hearing voices, made sense to my uncle. It defied logic. He got angry with me time and time again until one day I said that I had to leave (instead of just waiting for him to go to bed and sneaking off), and he finally gave in and told me, "Good luck". I attempted to run rather than walk and ended up in a small piece of land bordering the highway, where I thought I had laid in constant rain, unable to use my legs, for a few hours. I thought I was being told a few things. I had to 'Hoover' the earth. I had to inhale everything I saw: grass, trees, brick... everything. I tried to do it with a clump of weeds. I wasn't supposed to use my hands, but I cheated. I tried to press my face into the mud to smother myself. I tried to lodge a broken stick sticking out of the ground into my eye socket. Those few hours were actually a few days in the rain and mud. After a while, I imagined myself being able to break a large branch off of a fallen tree to use as a crutch but was unable to do so. It had finally stopped raining and the sun was out. I dragged myself on my knees, severely ripping the skin off of them, down the long hill and onto the street that my uncle lives on. I sat in the middle of the street drinking filthy water out of a pothole until a car passing that notified 911 and had the police sent over to rescue me. They believed I was homeless, but I somehow indicated that I lived with my uncle who was only about a block away. I was fearful of being brought to him, however, since I left and he was visibly and vocally fed up with this mess.

It wasn't the first time that I had escaped from the house either. One time before that, I left and ran up behind the house into the wooded area behind it. There was a drainage pipe leading into a small stream. I had lost the use of my legs then too. I ended up rolling into the water where I sat, trying to swallow seaweed and rocks. I succeeded with some seaweed and one rock. I was found by neighbors, choking on a rock that I couldn't squeeze down my throat.

On both occasions, I was taken to the hospital where I would try to escape or simply sign myself out. The first time, I was told directly that I could die if I left. I didn't care. I had to be in court. The voices told me so. They called my uncle to pick me up but didn't tell him that I signed myself out. The second time, I was put into a hospital. I don't know how long I was there. They wanted to insert a catheter and I was adamantly refusing for a long time. Finally, they persuaded me to let them do it.

I got relocated to a nursing home / rehabilitation center. My knees were scraped raw, and they wouldn't let me leave until they were healed enough to not get infected. I was re-regulated on medications and was there for two months. Meanwhile, a new court case appeared. My fear had become a reality. I was doomed to endlessly be tied in court cases. A divorce and a lawsuit with the company were about to get rolling and I wasn't in a state of mind to deal with either one.

Since August of 2022, I have only had two months where I have not experienced a schizophrenic episode of some degree. It is currently March 15, 2025 as I write this. As time passes, I am more frequently experiencing episodes. I see a psychiatrist once a month, and with the best efforts possible have remained on my medications, but I have missed a few days here and there, which typically causes an episode to occur. Almost every time I get off of a call concerning my court case, I have an episode. Everything I do that I feel guilty about seems to trigger one – even if all I did was display a little more happiness than I believe I should be allowed to show. I will try to explain these episodes in more detail in a bit.

Disabled

In February of 2022, I left my job with the company that is currently taking me to court. My family took the steps necessary to get me put on Social Security Disability. I was still in the hospital in July of 2022 when I received the award letter and began receiving payments in August.

While the amount of money that I receive on disability is not much, I have reduced my debt by a considerable amount, with some help. I now have a couple hospital bills, a car payment, and a few smaller temporary bills that are manageable. I am more wealthy (have more money available) now than at any other time in my life - but I don't have enough to have a place of my own, even though my debt is less than $40,000.

I am greatly blessed that my uncle provides me a place to stay. Nobody else was going to let me in that I know of. I might have been able to find a place with a roommate, but I never explored that route. I do know that I cannot live by myself due to my mental condition.

As a Lover – Part 3

Before this schizophrenic episode, I began to talk to a girl I met in the video game I played. It started out really rough. We both drank a lot, so, when two people that can get argumentative when they consume alcohol start talking to each other, only true love blossoms! As time passed, however, we grew to like each other to the point we confessed that we were meant to be together. It would be a 'relationship' that lasted quite a long time, but it never developed to the point where we'd meet in real life.

I believed wholeheartedly, especially after the divorce, that we would eventually meet and live happily ever after. Then, I started playing a different video game and left the one that had been our meeting place. I prepared a computer for her so that we could continue to play the same games together and have our chances to talk to each other, but she never got around to getting up and running. The chances to chat are barely there, but we do still communicate... just nearly not enough.

I strongly believe today that there isn't a woman out there waiting for me anymore. I don't know if I ever want to go through with another attempt of love that leads to marriage. I am uncertain if there could be a woman out there who would want to give me a chance after finding out this much about me. I don't have a whole hell of a lot to offer anyone at that capacity.

The Lawsuits

Dissolution

This whole divorce thing started out with good intentions. We were going to use it to better our lives together, I thought. There are things in life that come simpler for a person that is single than when they are married, or so we thought. It could be fictitious, I never googled it.

Our marriage, however, did take a turn for the worst at the tail end of our relationship. Accompanied by my waking up in a schizophrenic state that frightened my family, I believe that divorce was inevitable. I strongly believe that I was taken advantage of during a time when I was as vulnerable as I could ever be, though. My divorce papers state that I can only have supervised supervision of my daughter. Those supervised visits are supposed to be provided by only members of my ex-wife's family. Those visits started out being twice a week and dwindled to twice a month if I was lucky. I recently lashed out at not being able to see her as often as I should, which has so far, increased my visits to once a week. I am happier than I was, but I still feel left out of the life of my daughter. I don't get to see her on holidays. I don't get to see her on her birthday. She's turned 15 and I have missed out on so much already. Soon, she will blossom into adulthood and the time that she will have available to see me will probably be even less. I know I can have a great relationship with her. The love is still there. But with each year, the separation between a parent and their child that life forces upon families by the world inevitably inches closer.

I disliked some of how life was when I was married. I have a lot to say about it, but at the same time, I don't hate my ex-wife. Whether our feelings are a façade or true nature, we still get along like adults. Only time will tell. We can have moments of sternness that should probably be there, but at the same time, we can talk about the weather and other daily life things.

The Big Deal

I am currently involved in an ongoing confidential commercial court case as a defendant who also has counterclaims. I am wanting to publish a future book that will encompass my life beginning at age 48 and detail my current private life situations and detail my court case including the dealings with the company that led up to the court case... and perhaps include some other independent literary works that I feel are worthy of reading and what they mean to me.

Schizophrenia - Since the Lawsuits Began

I have been following everything political since a few months before Trump's first assassination attempt. Some of these episodes are loosely tied to conversations I've had on social media relating to arguments about it. I am only going to talk about three of them, but there are dozens of episodes that I have had. Some episodes started simply because of feelings of anger or happiness, dealing with my court cases.

Refund On Life

I've been going head to head against liberal Democrats for quite some time. I've kept in the loop with most of what is going on, and I have seen the same story and how it plays out across the multiverse. (the original, the left's version, the right's version).

One argument was with someone that later simply claimed that they aren't for Democrats or Republicans. He was simply 'woke'. Before I was privy to that fact, I figured he was a Democrat liberal bashing on Trump supporters. Regardless, he was bashing on Trump supporters. I argued up and down with this guy in a thread dedicated to incite violence between all of us. One guy popped a link to some theory concocted by a far-left leaning media outlet talking about the Two Santas.

The whole thing basically told of how the left and the right actually, behind closed doors, play off of each other on purpose. One Santa (the democrats) would tax and spend, and then the other Santa would deliver tax cuts.

There is a secondary economic standard that Republicans could leverage in this Santa scenario that would make it extremely difficult for a Democrat to gain the presidency. So, I read all of this stuff and was feeling really bad for bashing EVERYBODY.

I began spreading this link to a lot of the fights I was in in various threads and sending it to people in my friends list.

I told the guy that I was arguing with that I was extremely sorry. I shared the link. And he simply said that he isn't left or right, but woke, and wouldn't read that crap. I told him that from that point on, I would not bash anyone about this stuff ever again, and told him that I demanded a refund on life and wanted the fuck out. He simmered down too, and was trying to rationalize with me about perhaps voting Independent, since now we were somewhat agreeing that Democrats and Republicans both suck, more or less.

The moment I said that I wanted my refund, the room grew absolutely silent. I couldn't hear a thing. I got unplugged from the Matrix and was open game. And then I heard voices that I was committing treason by sharing that link. I got up from my chair as fast as I could and went to my room after wandering about aimlessly for a minute.

I tried to go to bed and force myself to sleep - incapable of closing my eyes. I sat there curled up in a ball, tossing from one side to the other, back and forth... probably every three minutes. I probably spent about three hours that way then finally bolted out of bed and was making my way out the door to the front porch. It was cold outside, and I was in my shorts and t-shirt with no coat or shoes. This is typical when I get this far.

My uncle came out behind me a moment later yelling at me that I didn't take my meds. He was trying to get me to take them, and the whole time, I was hearing voices telling me that that is a cop-out. It wouldn't work. They were on to me.

After a few times demanding that I take my medication, I went inside with my pills and took a dose. I didn't know how many doses I missed. It was three days' worth of meds. I take meds in the morning and at bedtime. I had missed three days worth because I would be so glued to the screen slamming people on Facebook day-in and day-out that I would snooze my alarms and forget to take them.

My uncle told me that he was going to make sure that I caught up with all of those doses… like a dose every two hours or so. By the time I took my next dose, I was calming back down to normal. By the time I took the last dose, I didn't feel like anything bad had happened at all.

I was back to normal - free to start bashing again. Nobody believed the drivel that was contained in the words provided in the linked website… including me. I found my trust back in with the Trump party, donned my helmet and rifle, and started battling it out with the liberal agenda once more.

SecDef

I know this episode started out with my usual liberal bashing, but I don't remember what I said or did, though that triggered it. All I know is that the world stopped making noise and I heard a voice in my head. The voice in my head identified itself as the Secretary of Defense… just SecDef.

I don't remember too much of what was happening or what I was hearing, but it was a bad trip episode. I believed that my cousin who was getting ready to retire from the Coast Guard was in on the conversation, on the SecDef's side. This, coincidentally, occurred only a few days before a few of us were about to fly out to see my cousin for a week for his retirement ceremony.

I couldn't make out any words. I could hear the police scanner going off left and right. The voices that were coming out of the TV in the living room didn't sound like the typical voices that I sometimes heard when my uncle was watching TV.

I had failed to take my medications once more. This time, it was a single day's doses. I finally took them, and within an hour or two, I was fine again. The fact that I can't even miss a single dose is beginning to scare the fuck out of me because it is seeming to me that I can have an episode triggered by the simplest of things.

Know My Number

The left were trying to push the narrative that Elon Musk and DOGE were going to gain access to all of the American people's social security numbers and other private information, including banking information.

I was on Facebook and there was a post about it and people were going nuts. I was reading through the ridiculous messages inside and said I was fine with Elon having my info, how little money I have, and how I spend it. I stated that if he saw my information, he might feel sorry for me and give me a little jingle.

Suddenly, I began seeing ads or posts in rapid-fire succession: guitars, Marshall amplifiers, racing kits for game consoles, and even a Lamborghini Countach - my teenage dream car. I fell into an instant feeling of fear that I was being watched and that 'they' knew everything about me and that they were tuned in to my current thoughts and actions.

I bolted to my room and was able to eventually sleep off the attack. I had missed a single dose that I took before going to my room and attempting to fall asleep.

The Pattern

I've been trying to piece all of this stuff together. It's a little difficult, but I think I am beginning to notice a pattern. One, and this is a scary one… if I don't take my medicine every day, it seems I am very susceptible to an episode. Where I could go a decade or more without having a single incident, I am now having them if I miss a day or more of doses. It's scary. The next thing that I am noticing is that there has to be some type of trigger. For these more recent episodes, it seems to be some kind of strong emotion being triggered by my interactions online. And finally, I am thinking that my sleep cycle may be involved. I can spend many hours on the internet before going to sleep, and by the time I go to bed, it isn't long before I wake up again and repeat the cycle.

I mentioned it earlier, but the strange thing about these episodes, depending on how severe they are, I don't recall that I have schizophrenia. At least, not at first. If someone, like my uncle, confronts me with my medications, for example, it starts to make sense, but the fact that I have schizophrenia is elusive to my mind.

I should call the doctor that prescribes my medicine and ask her for her thoughts. Should I perhaps have the dosages increased? I just saw her a few weeks ago and didn't think to ask her. I will call and find out what she thinks.

When I am asked about how I feel about my court stuff, I tell people that it doesn't bother me at all. It's not entirely accurate, as I can get very heated during the discussions taking place, but when the video goes dead, so do my thoughts about it. Maybe those thoughts aren't going away; I just repress them. I'm no psychologist. I'll talk to the big guy, next meeting.

As a Parent – Part 2

I can only be the best dad that I can be from this day forward. If I can't see her face-to-face, there is a world of technology at my disposal. I want the very best for her, and she deserves to be able to look at me without an ounce of hatred. I know that there has to be a level of unseen resentment behind those blue eyes though. I can only hope that with time, that level decreases and more love fills the void left inside.

Its hard. Its difficult to find things to discuss with a girl that seemingly only yesterday was learning to read and write. And while I did play with her and paid attention to everything she did, at the same time, I feel as though the gaps that were there have somehow removed a lot of space for conversation. What is it that interests her today? What are her ambitions for tomorrow? Are they the same as they were yesterday? I find myself talking about the same things repeatedly, just to make conversation. It's not that bad, but I just feel that way. Am I interesting? Am I showing enough interest? I have doubts about myself.

She always seems happy to see me though. I can't deny myself that fact. As long as she is happy to see me, I will be there waiting for her smiles. The day that that stops, I won't know what to do with the rest of my life. I hope that that day never comes.

There are so many things that I want to have her see in the world, without fears. She's been coddled for so long that I believe she's not wanting to step out into the unknown world. The exploring nature that I always had doesn't seem to exist within her, and while she has an imagination that is impressive, she has seen so little to inspire herself with. I know that right now, I couldn't get her to go on an airplane to visit some faraway land or to get on a boat and sail the seas. But maybe, I can get her to go wherever she would like to go, whenever she wants to go there with me tagging along.

I love her with all my heart, and I hope that some of the changes that I want to make with my own life, and the challenges that I MUST overcome will allow me to be for her now, more than I have ever been before.

Outcomes

One of my cousins calls me a Negative Nancy. I don't believe that to be true. Yes, I will talk negatively about my past, but what he might not think to himself is... I cope. I don't let my past burden me, but use it to leap forward. I have no intention of ever living in a state of anxiety, fear, depression, hatred, or doubt.

Only after losing the ability to gain employment have I invested largely into the things that I should have always been deeply intertwined. I am learning the latest toolkits and platforms for software development. I am also learning more about mobile development. I know more about Android Development now than I ever did 'doing it for a living'. I have delved deeply into 3D modeling, animation, and special effects – game development, etc. I have begun taking guitar lessons – started about a year and half ago as a coping mechanism for my schizophrenia and to play more sophisticated styles. I have been playing guitar since 1987 and still believe that I suck at it. I am learning though. I have more skills now in a little over a year of lessons than I have trying to learn it on my own for decades, and am now on my way to actually composing a song of my very own - and my instructor loves it.

I have a better relationship with my daughter. I don't believe I ever had a bad relationship with her, but I feel as though I wasn't there for her nearly as much as I should have been. I want to make up for that lost time and am just hoping that I am afforded the chance.

My only chance of success moving forward would be to create something entirely on my own. I have been out of the industry for so long that nothing short of a large investment in time and money to show that I have invested in myself will ever get me back in. I could be wrong, but just like with this corrupt company, I would be conducting a large number of interviews with the hopes of sparking an interest in just one of them.

There is nothing I can do about the divorce anymore. I can't fight the words that have been signed off on those pages. I can, however, challenge any wrongdoings moving forward. I have made that known. I choose to accomplish fairness as individuals rather than resorting to an act of war in the courtroom. I am only hoping that civility can be maintained until such a time when that side of the family no longer needs to be accommodating in any way.

Alcohol has taken a toll on me, not only in the past with mistakes and possibly a device that aided in schizophrenic outbreaks but also physically. I have developed fatty liver, which is a stage of damage preceding cirrhosis. I am very lucky that my indulgence in alcohol hasn't severed any family ties. That can happen to people. I do know that I might have given people reasons to either laugh at me or get upset at times. At the rate of which I consumed alcohol, I would strongly suggest not following in my footsteps. All it is is a path to hell, in every possible fashion.

If you liked this condensed history of my life, stay tuned for the next chapter… it could be a year from now… it could be a very long time from now… and hopefully, it will make this story feel like a pivotal situation to A BETTER LIFE BEYOND FIFTY.

If you made it this far, thank you very much for taking the time to learn more about me. Please visit my website: **https://cruckman.com**. There, you can view some other interesting things that I do, like 3D modeling. I have links set up where you can find me on Facebook, X,

LinkedIn, etc. Don't be shy. See you in the next chapter!

Friendly Advice For Those Who Drink

I would say this for people who do illicit drugs too, but I am not well-versed in that beat.

I'm currently 51 years old. I have been drinking, if I count my first beer, since the age of 14. I didn't kick start my gig until I was 20 and just kept rocking it hardcore from there.

I have done a ton of damage to myself, as is evident in this book. Part of the reason I wanted to craft this book was to display to others just where the path leads when you follow the bottle. I don't think I even mentioned how much damage I have done to my body, my liver. I have Fatty Liver. It sounds funny saying it, but it is a precursor to Cirrhosis. Cirrhosis is fatal. So, with some grace of God, I am not dying just yet.

Nobody can tell you what to do. All anyone can do is show enough love and compassion for you and hope that you take the words in earnest. Find your own intervention. My uncle was mine. When everything in my life came to a screeching halt, he was there to pick up my pieces, but the only condition he had was, no alcohol. I've failed him on that a bit, but I am learning. Learning is tough, but so is love. Follow your heart.

I have replaced most of my alcoholic beverages with coffee and zero-sugar sodas. None of it is as good for you as pure water, but let's be honest... nobody really enjoys pure water. Some will say amicably that they do, but they are lying to your face. Water is odorless and tasteless. What is there about water to enjoy... really? Skip a beer, drink a tea or even the blah water. Minimize the amount of alcohol you consume. Unlike me at my highest point, you can wake up in the morning and not have a beer. You CAN go through your day without a beer constantly wrapped in your hands. Before bed, make sure you brush your teeth and maybe have a glass or two of water to help cleanse some of the alcohol from your body.

Your health is important. The older you get, the more you will appreciate cutting back, if you are unable to cut it out completely.

Friendly Advice For the Mentally Ill or Their Caretakers

I can only speak to schizophrenia sufferers and the people that are in their sphere. It is a tough illness. Not knowing what is real, even when people are telling you that what you are witnessing is something made up in your head, is very scary. When you can't even trust the person that brought you into this world, that is a scary place indeed. Something that I want to try, for myself and perhaps with my uncle's help, is to make handwritten signs to look at when I am having an episode. Maybe it will help me convince myself to seek help. If my uncle sees me in a bad situation, perhaps he can pull out a note or sign that I made, that I can recognize, and maybe… that might be strong enough to pull me back out of the void.

I don't know if I will ever be able to live entirely on my own. I've never had to. The moment I left the nest, I was surrounded by friends and had roommates. I've never lived on my own. So, what would happen if I am all alone and I have an episode like I was when I had my very first one? That first episode was Disney on Ice compared to the shit I go through now. I've contemplated suicide. I have sat at the edge of the couch thinking I heard voices telling me, "If you go outside right now completely naked, you will go to jail and not have to go to court". I hesitate. The voice says, "Too late, now you gotta rob a bank, but you have to unlock everything with your tongue". "Too late. Now you gotta murder somebody". See where this could go?

So, if you are the one suffering from this illness, make sure you stay on your medications, always. I set alarms on my phone… I just need to actually make sure I take them when the alarm goes off before I forget again. If you can, identify some of the things that may adversely trigger you - heightened emotions, stress, and freedoms might cause an episode to occur. Find a way, that if you can't indicate and control the onset of an episode, to pull yourself back to reality. As I said above, I am going to try to hand write messages that I feel could ground me in the real world.

If you are someone that is taking care of someone with this illness, be loving and compassionate, but realize, there could be times when you have to be very firm in your actions and your voice. You can't roll over and play dead on this one. Try to identify the trends of the illness - what behaviors are prevalent when the person is having an episode? Are they distant, overly passive or aggressive, do they exhibit any kind of noticeable differences from their normal behavior?

I have never been around that is in a constant schizophrenic state. I only speak on what I know about myself. The people closest to me know all the signs and symptoms, so I know that it isn't hard to identify issues and formulate plans to combat the onset of an episode.

If all else fails, find a hospital that has the facilities to handle a person with mental illness. If this is occurring regularly, try different hospitals until you find the one that produces the best results. And, keep in mind, most visits are going to be voluntary out-patient. That means that the individual is free to sign themselves out at any time. Be aware of their conditions and behaviors. In doing this, you can be assured that you will be minimizing the potential for them to harm themselves and others, and hopefully get the treatment that they need to 'snap out of it'.

Make it a practice to continually educate the person with the illness. Speaking to a therapist is perhaps the most effective way, but any medium can be used to help them understand their condition. The more that they are made aware of, the easier it may be to confront them when they are at the lowest states of their existence. I came from a very dark state that lasted the better part of a year. It took a whole lot of understanding on many people's hands to recreate me.

Friendly Advice For Future Job Seekers

If you are out there looking for a job and you get an interview with some company that you don't know about already, research them. Don't simply go to their website and read their mission statement. DIG for information. Find out if they are truly legit. Find out how past and present employees rate the company and the CEO. Read their comments and any threads tied to them. I highly recommend https://www.glassdoor.com. You can perform searches for employers on there and get some good information. Don't stop there. Google search to see if they are a scam or fraudulent. If you feel somewhat safe to take the interview, gauge that interview process. Was it par for the course, or could a preschooler pass it? There may be a few instances where the interview process is simple, but the chances are very rare. Once you pass the interview, if you take it, and are presented with a contract to sign (if that is how they do things), read it thoroughly. If you don't understand it, consult a lawyer. NEVER let them dictate to you what is contained in that contract. It is your right to read it. It is your right to present it to a lawyer for interpretation before signing it.

Friendly Advice on Love

Read or write her poetry. Play her her favorite songs. Take her to her favorite places. But above all, don't take advice from me. All that stuff I just said is nothing more than the basic givens.

Where Life Takes You

I have always believed that I lived a great life… until I started to put a majority of it to paper. I have lived a life with a lot of happiness, but like many around me, with quite a bit of pain and suffering as well. I detail moments in my life and the tragedies that have put me where I exist today. Prepare to go on a journey full of pain with me.

www.ingramcontent.com/pod-product-compliance
Lightning Source LLC
LaVergne TN
LVHW101441200926
848483LV00001B/11
9781805588245